ELITE SERII

EDITOR: MARTIN WI

South-East Asian Special Forces

Text by KENNETH CONBOY

Colour plates by SIMON McCOUAIG

OSPREY PUBLISHING LONDON

Published in 1991 by
Osprey Publishing Ltd
59 Grosvenor Street, London, W1X 9DA
© Copyright 1991 Osprey Publishing Ltd

British Library Cataloguing in Publication Data
Conboy, Kenneth
    South-East Asian special forces. – (Elite series,
    no. 33).
    1. Soviet special forces
    I. Title II. Series
    356.160959

    ISBN 1-85532-106-8

Filmset in Great Britain
Printed through Bookbuilders Ltd, Hong Kong

Artist's Note

Readers may care to note that the original paintings
from which the colour plates in this book were
prepared are available for private sale. All reproduc-
tion copyright whatsoever is retained by the publisher.
All enquiries should be addressed to:
    Simon McCouaig
    4 Yeoman's Close
    Stoke Bishop
    Bristol BS9 1DH

The publishers regret that they can enter into no
correspondence upon this matter.

Author's Note

I would like to thank the following who generously
gave of their time in compiling this study: Doan Huu
Dinh, Tran Dac Tran, Hiep Hoa Trinh, Thoai
Hovanky, Southay Vongsavanh, Oroth Insisien-
gmay, Albert Grandolini, Thach Saren, Thach Reng,
the Indonesian Embassy (Washington), the Malaysian
Embassy (Washington), the Royal Thai Embassy
(Washington), the Embassy of the Philippines (Washington), the Singaporean Embassy (Washington), and
countless others who would rather remain anonymous.
Elite units have long been prominent in the armies of
South-East Asia, and, given the turmoil in the region
since the 1960s these forces have had ample opportun-
ity to be tested in combat. For reasons of space the
author has been obliged to exclude such units as the
South Vietnamese Airborne and Ranger formations;
but see Elite 29, *Vietnam Airborne* by Gordon L. Rott-
man for details of these units. Additional information
on Cambodian élite units can be found in MAA 209
The War in Cambodia.

Republic of Vietnam: Special Forces

In early 1956 the French-built Commando School at Nha Trang was re-established with US military assistance to provide physical training and ranger instruction for up to 100 students. Early the following year President Ngo Dinh Diem ordered the creation of a special unit to conduct clandestine external operations. Initial parachute and communication training for 70 officers and sergeants was conducted at Vung Tau; 58 of these later underwent a four-month commando course at Nha Trang under the auspices of a US Army Special Forces Mobile Training Team. Upon completion, they formed the *Lien doi Quan Sat so 1* (1 Observation Unit) on 1 November 1957 at Nha Trang. The unit was put under the Presidential Liaison Office, a special intelligence bureau controlled by President Diem and outside the normal ARVN command structure. The commander was Lt.Col. Le Quang Tung, an ARVN airborne officer and Diem loyalist. Many of the Unit's members came originally from northern Vietnam, reflecting its external operations orientation.

In 1958 the Unit was renamed the *Lien Doan Quan Sat so 1*, or 1 Observation Group, reflecting its increase to nearly 400 men in December. By that time the Group was seen as an anti-Communist stay-behind force in the event of a North Vietnamese conventional invasion; however, because of its privileged position the Group stayed close to Diem and rarely ventured into the field.

By 1960 it was apparent that the main threat to South Vietnam was growing Viet Cong insurgency; the Group abandoned its stay-behind role and was assigned missions in VC-infested areas. Operations were briefly launched against VC in the Mekong Delta, and later along the Lao border.

ARVN STD 'Earth Angel' team dressed in North Vietnamese uniforms prepare for insertion into Cambodia, 1971.

STD team members dressed in tiger-stripe fatigues practise communications skills at Camp Yen The, 1971.

In mid-1961 the Group had 340 men in 20 teams of 15, with plans for expansion to 805 men. In October the Group began operations into Laos to reconnoitre North Vietnamese Army logistical corridors into South Vietnam. In November the Group was renamed *Lien Doan 77*, or 77 Group, in honour of its USSF counterparts. Over the next two years members were regularly inserted into Laos and North Vietnam on harassment and psychological warfare operations. Longer-duration agent missions, involving civilians dropped into North Vietnam, also came under the Group's auspices.

The Group's sister unit, 31 Group, began forming in February 1963. Following criticism of 77 Group's perceived role as Diem's 'palace guard', both groups were incorporated into a new command, the *Luc Luong Dac Biet* (LLDB) or Special Forces, on 15 March 1963. In theory the LLDB would work closely with the USSF in raising irregular village defence units. This cosmetic change still kept the Special Forces outside of ARVN control, however, and did little to change the performance of Col. Tung's troops. In August, LLDB members attacked Buddhist pagodas across South Vietnam in an effort to stifle Buddhist opposition to the Diem regime. At the time LLDB strength stood at seven companies, plus an additional three 'civilian' companies used by Diem on political operations. Because of such missions the LLDB became despised and, when anti-Diem military units staged a coup d'état in November, the rebel forces arrested Col. Tung

and quickly neutralized the LLDB. (Tung was later executed.)

The LLDB after Diem

In the wake of the coup the Presidential Liaison Office was dissolved and its functions assumed by the ARVN. The LLDB was put under the control of the Joint General Staff and given the mission of raising paramilitary border and village defence forces with the USSF. External operations were given to the newly formed Liaison Service, also under the JGS. The Liaison Service, commanded by a Colonel, was headquartered in Saigon adjacent to the JGS. It was divided into Task Forces 1, 2, and 3, each initially composed of only a small cadre of commandos.

In 1964 the JGS also formed the Technical Service, a covert unit tasked with longer-duration agent operations into North Vietnam. Commanded by a lieutenant-colonel, the Technical Service comprised Group 11, oriented toward agent operations in Laos and eastern North Vietnam; Group 68, another infiltration unit; and the Coastal Security Service, a maritime commando group at Da Nang with its own contingent of PT Boats for seaborne infiltration.

The post-Diem LLDB was restructured for its proper role as a source of counter-insurgency instructors for paramilitary forces. By February 1964 31 Group had finished training, and was posted to Camp Lam Son south of Nha Trang. In May the Group became responsible for all LLDB detachments in I and II Corps. A second reorganization occurred in September when 31 Group was renamed 111 Group and given responsibility for the Special Operations Training Center at Camp Lam Son. Now 77 Group, headquartered at Camp Hung Vuong in Saigon, became 301 Group. In addition, 91 Airborne Ranger Battalion, a three-company fast reaction para unit, was raised under LLDB auspices in November. Total LLDB force strength stood at 333 officers, 1,270 sergeants, and 1,270 men. The LLDB command at Nha Trang was assumed by Brig.Gen. Doan Van Quang in August 1965.

By 1965 the LLDB had become almost a mirror image of the USSF. LLDB Headquarters at Nha Trang ran the nearby Special Forces Training Center at Camp Dong Ba Tinh. LLDB 'C' Teams, designated A through D Company, were posted to each of South Vietnam's four Military Regions; each 'C' Team had three 'B' Teams, which controlled operational detachments at the sub-regional level; 'B' Teams ran 10 to 11 'A' Teams. 'A' Teams were co-located with USSF 'A' Teams at camps concentrated along the South Vietnamese border, where they focused on training Civilian Irregular Defense Force (CIDG) personnel.

In addition, the LLDB Command directly controlled Delta teams and the four-company 91 Airborne Ranger Battalion, both used by Project Delta, a special reconnaissance unit of the US Military Assistance Command-Vietnam Studies and Observation Group (MACVSOG), which operated deep in VC/NVA sanctuaries.

On 30 January 1968 the Communists launched their Tet offensive across South Vietnam. Caught celebrating the lunar New Year, the Saigon government was initially ill-prepared to counter the VC/NVA attacks. When Nha Trang was hit on the first day the LLDB Headquarters was protected by 91 Airborne Ranger Battalion, recently returned from one of its Project Delta assignments. At only 60 per cent strength the

Airborne Rangers turned in an excellent performance, pushing the major Communist elements out of Nha Trang in less than a day. The battle, however, cost the life of the battalion commander and wounded four company commanders.

After a four-month retraining phase in Nha Trang three companies from 91 Airborne Ranger Battalion were brought together with six Delta teams and renamed 81 Airborne Ranger Battalion. In early June the new battalion prepared for urban operations in Saigon after a second surge of Communist attacks pushed government forces out of the capital's northern suburbs. On 7 June the Airborne Rangers were shuttled into Saigon and began advancing toward VC-held sectors around the Duc Tin Military School. After a week of bloody street fighting, much of it at night, the Rangers pushed the enemy out of the city.

Following the Tet Offensive 81 Airborne Ranger Battalion was increased to six companies, and continued to be used as the main reaction force for Project Delta; four companies were normally assigned Delta missions while two remained in reserve at LLDB Headquarters.

The Strategic Technical Directorate

In late 1968 the Technical Service was expanded into the *Nha Ky Thuat* (Strategic Technical Directorate, or STD) in a move designed to make it more like MACVSOG, the US joint-services command created in 1964 which ran reconnaissance, raids, and other special operations both inside and outside South Vietnam. Despite internal opposition the Liaison Service was subordinated to the STD as its major combat arm. Like SOG, the STD also had aircraft under its nominal

A stick from the Laotian 1 CCPL prepare for a training jump from a French AAC-1 'Toucan', early 1950. (ECPA)

control, including 219 Helicopter Squadron of the Vietnamese Air Force. By the late 1960s the size of the Liaison Service had increased tremendously. Task Forces 1, 2, and 3—commanded by lieutenant-colonels and larger than a brigade—were directly analogous to MACVSOG's Command and Control North, Central, and South. Each Task Force was broken into a Headquarters, a Security Company, a Reconnaissance Company of ten teams, and two Mobile Launch Sites with contingents of South Vietnamese Army and paramilitary forces under temporary Liaison Service control. Although the Liaison Service was a South Vietnamese unit, all of its operations were funded, planned, and controlled by MACVSOG, and recon teams integrated both MACVSOG and Liaison Service personnel.

In December 1970, in accordance with the 'Vietnamization' policy, all CIDG border camps were turned over to the South Vietnamese government and CIDG units were incorporated into the ARVN as *Biet Dong Quan*, or Ranger, border battalions. No longer needed as a CIDG training force, the LLDB was dissolved in the same month. Officers above captain were sent to the *Biet Dong Quan*; the best of the remaining officers and men were selected for a new STD unit, the Special Mission Service. At the same time 81 Airborne

French and Lao members of 1 CCPL in US-supplied World War Two Pacific camouflage uniforms engage the enemy with MAS36 rifles in what appears to be a posed publicity picture, February 1951. (ECPA)

Ranger Battalion was expanded into 81 Airborne Ranger Group consisting of one headquarters company, one recon company, and seven exploitation companies. The Group was put under the direct control of the Army G-2 (Intelligence).

During 1970 the Liaison Service had staged numerous cross-border missions into Cambodia in support of major external sweeps by the US and South Vietnamese forces against Communist sanctuaries. Early the following year the Service sent three recon teams into the 'Laotian Panhandle' two weeks before the ARVN's February *Lam Son 719* incursion.

In February 1971 the STD underwent major reorganization in accordance with Vietnamization and its anticipated increase in special operations responsibilities. Headquartered in Saigon, STD command was given to Col. Doan Van Nhu, an ARVN airborne officer and former military attaché to Taiwan. As STD commander, and a non-voting member of the South Vietnamese National Security Council, Nhu took orders only from President Nguyen Van Thieu and the Chief of the ARVN JGS.

The expanded STD consisted of a headquarters, a training center, three support services, and six combat services. The training center was located at Camp Yen The in Long Thanh; Yen The, significantly, was the name of a resistance movement in northern Vietnam during the 11th century. Airborne instruction was conducted at the ARVN Airborne Division' Camp Ap Don at Tan Son Nhut. The three support services were Administration & Logistics; Operations & Intelligence,

and Psychological Warfare, which ran the 'Vietnam Motherland', 'Voice of Liberty', and 'Patriotic Front of the Sacred Sword' clandestine radio stations. The combat services were the Liaison Service; the Special Mission Service; Group 11; Group 68; the Air Support Service; and the Coastal Security Service.

The Liaison Service, commanded by a colonel in Saigon, was composed of experienced Loi Ho ('Pull a tiger's tail') recon commandos divided among Task Force 1 (Da Nang), Task Force 2 (Kontum), and Task Force 3 (Ban Me Thuot).

The Special Mission Service, also commanded by a colonel, was headquartered at Camp Son Tra in Da Nang. It remained in training under US auspices from February 1971 until January 1972. Unlike the shorter-duration raid and recon missions performed by the Liaison Service, the SMS was tasked with longer missions into North Vietnam and Laos. It was initially composed of Groups 71, 72, and 75, the first two headquartered at separate camps at Da Nang. Group 75 was headquartered at Pleiku in the former LLDB 'B' Co. barracks, with one detachment at Kontum to provide a strike force for operations in Cambodia and inside South Vietnam.

Group 11, an airborne infiltration unit based at Da Nang, and Group 68, headquartered in Saigon with detachments at Kontum, were soon integrated under SMS command. Group 68 ran airborne-trained rallier and agent units, including 'Earth Angels' (NVA ralliers) and 'Pike Hill' teams (Cambodians disguised as Khmer Communists). A typical Earth Angel operation took place on 15 December 1971, when a team was inserted by US aircraft on a reconnaissance mission into Mondolkiri Province, Cambodia. Pike Hill operations were focused in the same region, including a seven-man POW recovery team dropped into Ba Kev, Cambodia, on 12 February 1971. Pike Hill operations even extended into Laos, e.g. the four-man Pike Hill team parachuted onto the edge of the Bolovens Plateau on 28 December 1971, where it reported on enemy logistics traffic for almost two months. Pike Hill operations peaked in November 1972 when two teams were inserted by C-130 Blackbird aircraft flying at 250 feet north of Kompong Trach, Cambodia. Information from one of these teams resulted in 48 B-52 strikes within one day.

The STD's Air Support Service consisted of 219 'Queen Bee' Helicopter Sqn., the 114 Observation Sqn., and C-47 transportation elements. The Queen Bees, originally outfitted with aging H-34s, were re-equipped with UH-1 Hueys in 1972. The C-47 fleet was augmented by two C-123 transports and one C-130 Blackbird in the same year. All were based at Nha Trang.

The Easter Offensive 1972

During the 1972 Easter Offensive the combat arms of the STD saw heavy action while performing recon and forward air

Members of Laotian 1 BPL during Operation 'Dampieres' north of Luang Prabang, September 1953. Unlike the US pattern worn by the CCPL, the BPL had new French 'lizard' pattern camouflage. (ECPA)

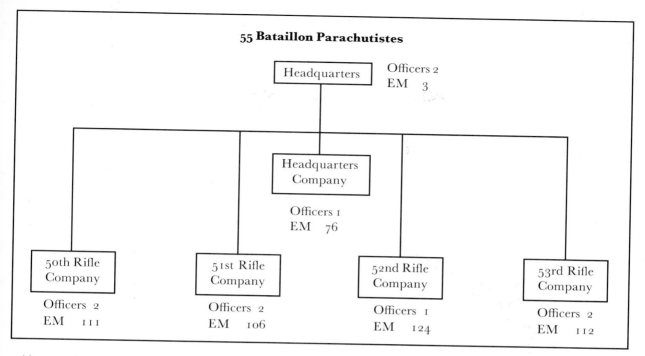

55 Bataillon Parachutistes

	Headquarters	Officers 2 EM 3

Headquarters Company

Officers 1
EM 76

50th Rifle Company	51st Rifle Company	52nd Rifle Company	53rd Rifle Company
Officers 2 EM 111	Officers 2 EM 106	Officers 1 EM 124	Officers 2 EM 112

guide operations. Meanwhile, 81 Airborne Ranger Group was tasked with reinforcing besieged An Loc. The Group was heli-lifted into the southern edge of the city in April, and the Rangers walked north to form the first line of defence against the North Vietnamese. After a month of brutal fighting and heavy losses, the siege was lifted. A monument was later built by the people of An Loc in appreciation of the Group's sacrifices.

In October 1972, the SMS was given responsibility for the tactical footage between Hue and the Lao border. In early 1973 US advisors were withdrawn. The Air Support Service soon proved unable to make up for missing US logistical support, sharply reducing the number of STD external missions. STD personnel, as well as LLDN SEALs, were increasingly seconded to President Thieu's Palace Guard. Later in the year the Liaison Service's Task Forces 1, 2, and 3 were redesignated Groups 1, 2, and 3; and Camp Yen The was renamed Camp Quyat Thang ('Must Win').

Following a brief respite in the wake of the 1973 Paris Peace Accords, the STD was back in action against encroaching NVA elements in the countryside. In September 1973 two Liaison Service *Loi Ho* recon teams were inserted by helicopter into Plei Djereng, a key garrison blocking the NVA infiltration corridor down the Western highlands. They were unsuccessful in rallying the defenders after an NVA attack, however.

In late 1974 the NVA increased their pressure; especially hard hit was the provincial capital of Phuoc Long in Military Region 3. After several weeks of NVA tank, artillery, and infantry attacks the Phuoc Long defences started to crack. In an effort to save the city the government ordered 81 Airborne

October 1954: Laotian para-commandos, probably from the GCPL just prior to its integration into the BPL, train near Vientiane. They wear Laotian Airborne red berets with badges based on the French Airborne winged dagger. Weapons are the BAR and Thompson SMG. (ECPA)

Organization of the Laotian 55 BP, 1961.

Ranger Group to reinforce the southern perimeter. After two days of weather delays one company was heli-lifted east of the city on the morning of 5 January 1975; and by early afternoon over 250 Airborne Rangers were in Phuoc Long. After a day of relentless NVA assaults most of the original garrison fled; contact was lost with the Airborne Rangers as the NVA began to overwhelm the city. Early the next day Ranger stragglers were spotted north of the city. A four-day search eventually retrieved some 50 per cent survivors.

By March 1975 the NVA had increased pressure on the Central Highlands, prompting Saigon to begin a strategic redeployment from the western half of II Corps. Although the Liaison Service's Groups 2 and 3 provided security for the withdrawing masses the redeployment soon turned into a rout. In the hasty withdrawal Group 2 had forgotten two recon teams in Cambodia; these later walked the entire distance back to the Vietnamese coast. After the fall of the Central Highlands government forces in I Corps began to panic, sparking an exodus to the south. In the confusion Group 1 of the Liaison Service attempted to provide security for the sealift to Saigon. Meanwhile, the SMS boarded boats on 30 March for Vung Tau.

With the entire northern half of the country lost, Saigon attempted to regroup its forces. 81 Airborne Ranger Group, which had arrived from II Corps in a state of disarray, was refitted at Vung Tau. The Liaison Service was posted in Saigon, with Groups 1 and 3 reinforcing Bien Hoa and Group 2 protecting the fuel depots. The SMS also re-formed in Saigon.

On 6 April 1975 SMS recon teams sent north-east and north-west of Phan Rang discovered elements of two North Vietnamese divisions massing on the city. An additional 100 SMS commandos were flown in as reinforcements, but were captured at the airport as the North Vietnamese overran

Phan Rang. A second task force of 40 *Loi Ho* commandos was infiltrated into Tay Ninh to attack an NVA command post; the force was intercepted and only two men escaped. By mid-April 81 Airborne Ranger Group was put under the operational control of 18th Division and sent to Xuan Loc, where the unit was smashed. The remnants were pulled back to defend Saigon. By the final days of April the NVA had surrounded the capital. Along with other high officials, the STD commander escaped by plane on 27 April. On the next day 500 SMS commandos and STD HQ personnel commandeered a barge and escaped into international waters. The remainder of the Liaison Service fought until capitulation on 30 April.

Vietnamese Naval Special Forces

In 1960 the South Vietnamese Navy proposed the creation of an Underwater Demolitions Team to improve protection of ships, piers, and bridges. Later in the year a navy contingent was sent to Taiwan for UDT training; the one officer and seven men who completed the course became the cadre for a *Lien Doi Ngoui Nhia* (LDNN), or Frogman Unit, formally established in July 1961. The LDNN, with a proposed strength of 48 officers and men, was given the mission of salvage, obstacle removal, pier protection, and special amphibious operations.

Insignia of the Laotian MR 5 Commandos, 1970.

Organization of the Khmer Special Forces, 1974.

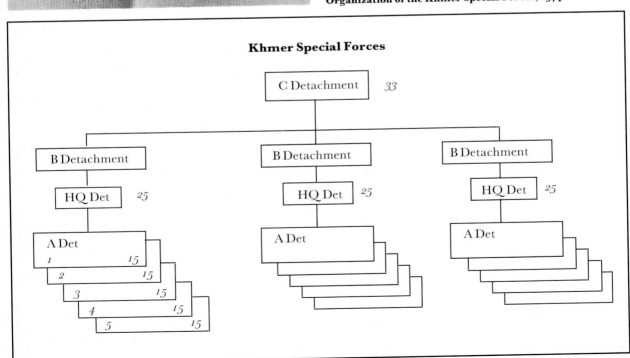

Khmer Special Forces

Indonesian KIPAM insignia: chest qualification badge (left); unit shoulder insignia and tab (centre); HALO qualification badge (right).

Soon after the creation of the LDNN a second unit was formed: *Biet Hai*, or 'Special Sea Force', paramilitary commandos under the operational control of Diem's Presidential Liaison Office and given responsibility for amphibious operations against North Vietnam. US Navy SEAL (Sea, Air, and Land) commando teams began deploying to South Vietnam in February 1962 and initiated in March a six-month course for the first *Biet Hai* cadre in airborne, reconnaissance, and guerrilla warfare training. By October, 62 men had graduated from the first cycle. A planned second contingent was denied funding.

In early 1964 the LDNN, numbering only one officer and 41 men, began special operations against VC seaborne infiltration attempts. Six Communist junks were destroyed by the LLDN at Ilo Ilo Island in January during Operation 'Sea Dog'. During the following month the LLDN began to be used against North Vietnamese targets as part of Operation Plan 34A, a covert action programme designed to pressure the Hanoi regime. In February a team unsuccessfully attempted to sabotage a North Vietnamese ferry on Cape Ron and Swatow patrol craft at Quang Khe. Missions to destroy the Route 1 bridges below the 18th Parallel were twice aborted. In March most of the LDNN was transferred to Da Nang and co-located with the remaining *Biet Hai* commandos. During May North Vietnam operations resumed by LDNN teams working with newly trained *Biet Hai* boat crews. On 27 May they scored their first success with the capture of a North Vietnamese junk. On 30 June a team landed on the North Vietnamese coast near a reservoir pump house. The team was discovered and a hand-to-hand fight ensued; two LDNN commandos lost their lives and three 57mm recoilless rifles were abandoned, but 22 North Vietnamese were killed and the pump house was destroyed.

In July a second class of 60 LDNN candidates was selected and began training in Nha Trang during September. Training lasted 16 weeks, and included a 'Hell Week' in which students were required to paddle a boat 115 miles, run 75 miles, carry a boat for 21 miles, and swim ten miles. During the training cycle team members salvaged a sunken landing craft at Nha Trang and a downed aircraft in Binh Duong Province. Thirty-three men completed the course in January 1965, and were based at Vung Tau under the direct control of the Vietnamese Deputy Chief of Naval Operations (Operations).

In 1965 the LLDN was given responsibility for amphibious special operations in South Vietnam. Maritime operations against North Vietnam were given exclusively to the Da Nang-based *Biet Hai* commandos and *Hai Tuan* boat crews, both incorporated into the new seaborne component of the STD, the *So Phong Ve Duyen Hai* (Coastal Security Service, or CSS). The CSS, a joint services unit, was headed by an Army lieutenant-colonel until 1966, then by a Navy commander. CSS missions focused almost entirely on short-duration sabotage operations lasting one night, and had a high success rate. The CSS relied heavily on special operations teams temporarily seconded from other services. Teams on loan from the Vietnamese Navy, considered most effective, were codenamed 'Vega'. Other teams came from the Vietnamese Marine Corps ('Romulus') and Army ('Nimbus'). The CSS also controlled 40 civilian agents ('Cumulus') until the mid-1960s. Unofficially, the term *Biet Hai* was used for all CSS forces, regardless of original service affiliation. CSS training was conducted at Da Nang under the auspices of US Navy SEAL, US Marine, and Vietnamese advisors. Further support was provided by the CSS's Da Nang-based US counterpart, the Naval Advisory Detachment, a component of MACVSOG.

By the mid-1960s US Navy SEAL teams were being rotated regularly through South Vietnam on combat tours. Specialists in raids, amphibious reconnaissance, and neutralization operations against the VC infrastructure, the SEALs worked closely with the LDNN and began qualifying Vietnamese personnel in basic SEAL tactics. In November 1966 a small cadre of LDNN were brought to Subic Bay in the Philippines for more intensive SEAL training.

In 1967 a third LDNN class numbering over 400 were selected for SEAL training at Vung Tau. Only 27 students finished the one-year course and were kept as a separate *Hai Kich* ('Special Sea Unit,' the Vietnamese term for SEAL) unit within the LDNN. Shortly after their graduation the Communists launched the Tet Offensive, and some of the young LDNN SEALs were sent to the Saigon district of Cholon for urban operations. In the wake of the Tet Offensive most of the LDNN SEALs were moved to Cam Ranh Bay, where a fourth LDNN class began training during 1968. During the year the Vietnamese SEALs operated closely with the US Navy SEALs. The LDNN SEAL Team maintained its focus on operations within South Vietnam, although some missions did extend into Cambodia. Some missions used parachute infiltration.

LDNN after Tet

In 1971, in accordance with increased operational responsibilities under the Vietnamization programme, the LDNN was expanded to the *Lien Doan Ngoui Nhia* (LDNN), or Frogman Group, comprising a SEAL Team, Underwater Demolitions Team, Explosive Ordnance Disposal Team, and Boat Support Team. Headquarters remained in Saigon. For the remainder of 1971 the SEALs operated in 12–18-man detachments on neutralization operations and raids inside South Vietnam. SEAL launch sites included Ho Anh, north of Da Nang; Hue; and Tinh An.

KIPAM team practising amphibious reconnaissance, armed with the AK-47.

During the 1972 Easter Offensive the SEALs were transferred to Hue to conduct operations against NVA forces holding Quang Tri; after Quang Tri was retaken some of the SEALs went to Quang Ngai to resume VC neutralization operations.

After US Navy SEAL advisors were withdrawn in late 1972 the LDNN SEAL Team, now 200 strong, took over training facilities at Cam Ranh Bay; training, however, was cut in half, with only one-fifth given airborne training. The SEALs had been augmented by ten graduates out of 21 LDNN officer candidates sent to the US for SEAL training in 1971.

When the Vietnam ceasefire went into effect in 1973 the SEALs returned to LDNN Headquarters in Saigon. At the same time the CSS was dissolved, with the Navy contingent given the option of transferring to the LDNN.

In late December 1973 the government reiterated its territorial claim to the Paracel Island chain off its coast and dispatched a small garrison of militia to occupy the islands. By early January 1974 the Chinese, who also claimed the islands, had sent a naval task force to retake the Paracels. On 17 January 30 LDNN SEALs were infiltrated on to the western shores of one of the major islands to confront a Chinese landing party. The Chinese had already departed; but two days later, after SEALs landed on a nearby island, Chinese forces attacked with gunboats and naval infantry. Two SEALs died and the rest were taken prisoner and later repatriated.

During the final days of South Vietnam a 50-man SEAL detachment was sent to Long Anh; the remainder were kept at LDNN Headquarters in Saigon along with 200 new SEAL trainees. During the early evening of 29 April all SEAL dependants boarded LDNN UDT boats and left Saigon; a few hours later the SEALs departed the capital, linked up with the UDT boats, and were picked up by the US 7th Fleet in international waters.

Cambodia: Army Airborne

In July 1947 the first Cambodian volunteers from the Mixed Cambodian Regiment were chosen for airborne training. Additional Cambodian paratroopers, totalling one company, were raised within the Cambodian Chasseur Battalion by 1951. In June 1952 these paratroopers were consolidated to form 1 Company of a planned Cambodian airborne battalion; second and third companies were soon formed and sent to Saigon for jump training. On 1 December all three companies were declared operational and the 1ᵉ Bataillon Parachutiste Khmere was officially created. As early as June 1952 1 Co. was engaging in small-scale clearing operations in southern Cambodia. By early 1953 both 1 and 2 Cos. were engaging Viet Minh elements. In July 1953 the entire BPK was sent to the north-eastern town of Sre Ches to drive out a Viet Minh battalion. On 31 August 1953 all French officers assigned to the Royal Cambodian Armed Forces, including the BPK, were withdrawn.

Following the August 1954 ceasefire in Indochina the BPK was used for small police actions against bands of armed rebels. During the latter half of the 1950s its authorized strength remained near 1,000 men; actual strength was closer to 900.

In January 1961 the battalion was expanded into the Airborne Half-Brigade, composed of 1 and 2 Para Battalions. Half-Brigade HQ and the airborne training centre were at Pochentong Airbase outside Phnom Penh. Aside from infrequent skirmishes along the South Vietnamese border—against both ARVN and VC forces—the paratroopers saw little action. In 1964 1 Para Bn. was parachuted near the Thai border in an effort to intimidate the Thai government during a dispute over control of the Preah Vihear temple. In April 1967 paratroopers were rushed to Battambang to put down the first armed uprising by the Communist Khmer Rouge movement.

In November 1969 elements of the Demi-Brigade were sent to the extreme north-east for limited sweeps against VC/NVA forces. At that time HQ and 1 Para Bn. were stationed at Pochentong; 2 Para Bn. was garrisoned at Long Vek. When Cambodian head of State Prince Norodom Sihanouk was deposed in March 1970 and replaced by a pro-Western republican government, the NVA attacked the isolated government forces in north-eastern Cambodia, forcing the paratroopers to evacuate to South Vietnam. They were subsequently retrained and sent back to Phnom Penh. During early April the remainder of the Demi-Brigade was rushed toward the South Vietnamese border to spearhead government offensives against VC/NVA enclaves in eastern Cambodia.

By August 1970, in accordance with plans for expansion of the Cambodian National Armed Forces, the airborne forces grew into an Airborne Brigade Group of two brigades. 1 Para Bde., based at Pochentong, was composed of a 188-man HQ Co. and five 577-man battalions (1, 2, 3, 4, and 5 Para Battalions). The first four had been quickly trained within Cambodia; 5 Para Bn. was sent for training in South Vietnam and did not return until February 1972. 2 Para Bde., based at Long Vek, started forming its first unit, 11 Para Bn., in late

KIPAM team practising ship infiltrations, 1986.

1970. Three further battalions—12, 13, and 14—were planned but only 12 Para Bn. was ever realized, completing South Vietnamese training and returning to the brigade in April 1972.

In late August 1970 the four existing battalions of 1 Para Bde. were sent to Prek Tameak nine miles north of Phnom Penh. For its two days of successful defensive action, the brigade was later awarded the Standard of Victory. In December 1 Bde. was sent to Prey Totung 44 miles north-east of Phnom Penh, where heavy fighting against NVA forces earned the brigade its second Standard.

In March 1971, after 101-D Regt. of the NVA 1st Division cut Route 4 leading to Kompong Som, the brigade was chosen to spearhead a drive to re-open the road. Over the next three months the paratroopers, supported by several infantry brigades, pushed back the NVA and eventually captured the strategic Pich Nil Pass overlooking Route 4. These actions earned the brigade its third Standard.

Indonesian PASKHAS team dressed in British DPM camouflage and armed with M-16s and an M-203.

The Airborne 1972-1975

In May 1972 three para battalions were moved from Phnom Penh to Siem Reap to participate in Operation 'Angkor Chey', a clearing action around the Angkor Wat temple. All three battalions were moved back to the capital in November.

In January 1973 paratroopers were fighting their way into Srey Prey, 37 miles south of Phnom Penh, to relieve a seriously threatened outpost. While the 4,000-strong Airborne Brigade Group remained active on similar reinforcement missions throughout early 1973, its combat performance was tinged with a lack of aggressiveness. In March 1 Para Bde. was assigned to clear and hold the east bank of the Mekong. After the operation extended beyond the promised five days, however, the brigade refused to move and began to desert its positions. The commander was relieved and the brigade was redeployed to the south Mekong. Tasked with advancing along the west bank, the paras again refused to move and started to filter back toward Phnom Penh.

As a result of its poor performance the Brigade Group was disbanded in April. 1 Para Bde., composed of 1, 2, 3, and 4 Para Bns., was retained with headquarters at Pochentong; 5 Para Bn. and 2 Para Bde., composed only of 11 and 12 Para Bns., were disbanded. During mid-1973 two para battalions were sent on operations along the Mekong River while two battalions. were maintained at Pochentong as a general reserve.

On 25 August, 1 and 3 Para Bns. were rushed to Kompong Cham following heavy Khmer Rouge attacks. All airborne forces were withdrawn from the vicinity of Kompong Cham in December and returned to Phnom Penh.

For the first six months of 1974 the paras were used on limited defensive operations along the east bank of the Mekong. Repeated enemy probes sapped the brigade's morale and brought strength down to 1,000 men. An infusion of 250 newly trained paratroopers in June improved performance slightly. During December elements of the brigade were sent to clear the banks of the Bassac River. The paratroopers were then sent east of the capital until mid-April 1975; the bulk of the brigade was finally rushed west of Phnom Penh on 15 April, but could only get six kilometres down Route 4 before the Khmer Rouge captured the capital two days later.

Khmer Special Forces

In October 1971 the Khmer Special Forces was created with an initial strength of one 33-man 'C' Detachment serving as headquarters in Phnom Penh; 1 Special Forces Group (Airborne), composed of one 25-man 'B' Detachment (B-11) and six 15-man 'A' Detachments (A-111 to A-116). Most members were Khmer Krom (a Cambodian ethnic minority living in southern Cambodia and southern Vietnam) who had been repatriated to Cambodia with years of combat experience in South Vietnamese élite units. In mid-1972 training began for 2 Special Forces Group (Airborne)—Detachment B-12 and Detachments A-121 to A-126—at the Royal Army Special Warfare Center at Lopburi, Thailand. Again, a large percentage of 2 Group were Khmer Krom repatriates.

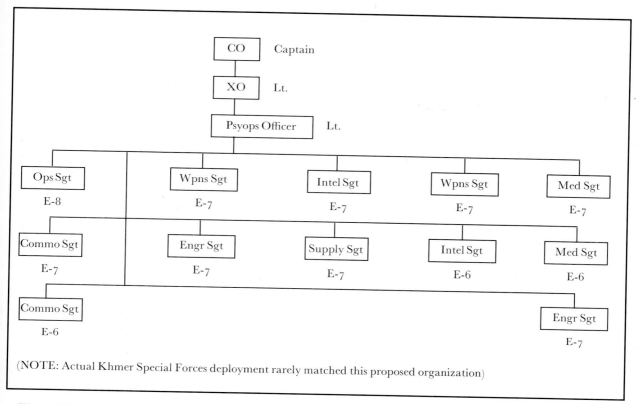

Khmer SF missions were varied. Its first combat assignment, clearing a Khmer Rouge rocket team from north of Phnom Penh, soon gave way to deep-penetration raids, long-range reconnaissance, and reinforcement duties. The SF also performed in an unconventional warfare training role for paramilitary units, as well as for Khmer Air Force security troops. In addition, SF personnel ran the Recondo School at Battambang.

In December 1972, 3 Special Forces Group (Airborne)—Detachment B-13 and Detachments A-131 to A-136—was brought to strength and sent to Lopburi for training. Unlike the previous two groups 3 Group had few experienced Khmer Krom members. On 23 April 1973 the Group graduated and returned to Cambodia. It was given responsibility for operations around the capital, along the lower Mekong, and the coast; 1 Group was posted to Battambang and 2 Group was stationed in Phnom Penh.

Though highly capable, the SF were too small to make a strategic difference in the war. Furthermore, some personnel were siphoned off to protect Phnom Penh from the threat of internal coups d'état, while two more 'A' Detachments were used for VIP security when President Lon Nol visited his villa on the coast.

The SF were augmented in late 1974 when they assumed operational control over the Para-Commando Battalion, a unit which had its origins in a 60-man contingent sent for nine months of Indonesian Special Forces training in March 1972. Upon their return 36 members were assigned to a ceremonial unit in Phnom Penh. Late in 1974, however, they were used as a cadre for a new Para-Commando Battalion and, under assignment to the Khmer SF, were sent to man the defensive perimeter north-west of the capital.

Organization of a Khmer Special Forces 'A' Detachment.

By March 1975 with all land and river routes to Phnom Penh cut, the Khmer Rouge began their final assault on the capital. Aside from three 'A' Detachments in Battambang and two in Siem Reap, the bulk of the Khmer SF were withdrawn to Phnom Penh. Two teams defended the national stadium, where seven escape helicopters were being kept to evacuate key members of the government. Only a handful of SF personnel managed to escape.

Laos

On 1 July 1948 3 Company of 1 Laotian Chasseur Battalion began airborne training and was renamed the 1ere Compagnie de Commandos Parachutistes Laotiens of the French Union Army. By September, 1 CCPL strength had risen to an HQ section and three commando sections, totalling 132 Laotians and 22 French. During the same month company headquarters was established at Wattay Airbase outside of Vientiane. On 11 May 1949, 1 CCPL performed its first operational parachute jump, dropping 18 commandos to reinforce the Nam Tha garrison. Six more airborne operations were conducted by the company during the year, including a 112-man jump to reinforce Sam Neua on 16 December.

On 29 April 1951 the company increased to six commando sections. In October, however, Commandos 4, 5, and 6 were removed to form 2 Co. of the new 1er Bataillon de Parachutistes Laotiens. The remainder of 1 CCPL conducted five

PASKHAS member dressed in DPM camouflage and armed with the folding-stock FNC. Note subdued rank insignia on chest tab, subdued 'Air Force' tab over left pocket, subdued unit insignia on left shoulder, and orange beret with distinctive PASKHAS badge.

airborne reinforcement jumps around the country during the year. On 1 March 1952 1 CCPL was renamed 1ere Compagnie de Commandos Laotiens (1 CCL). Numerous jumps were conducted during the year, mostly as part of counter-insurgency sweeps north of Vientiane.

On 27 April 1953 1 CCL was dropped at Nam Bac to establish a forward defensive line in the face of a Viet Minh invasion. The company was decimated, and could not reconstitute its headquarters section and four commando sections until 4 August. On 15 June 1954 the company was transferred from the French Union Army to the Laotian National Army, changing its name to 1ere Groupement de Commandos Parachutistes Laotiens. All French officers left the group by August.

A second Laotian parachute unit, the 1er Bataillon de Parachutistes Laotiens, began forming in October 1951. By 1 April 1952 the battalion was brought to strength with 853 men and officers, divided into a headquarters and three companies. Based at Chinaimo outside of Vientiane, 1 BPL participated in 20 operations, six involving parachute jumps, during 1952. On 15–24 December 576 members of the unit conducted a reinforcement drop into Sam Neua garrison during Operation 'Noel'. Eighty more members of the battalion jumped into Sam Neua in February 1953, enabling the BPL to create a fourth company.

On 15 April 1953, a massive Viet Minh invasion crushed the Sam Neua garrison and sent remnants of the BPL fleeing toward the Plain of Jars. A month later the battalion was reconstituted at Chinaimo. Recon and commando operations were conducted north of Luang Prabang for the remainder of the year.

In March 1954 the BPL began preparing for Operation 'Condor', the planned relief of the besieged Dien Bien Phu garrison in North Vietnam. During April and early May the battalion moved toward the Lao-Vietnamese border, but was withdrawn in mid-May after the garrison fell. On 18 June the BPL regrouped at Seno, a French airbase near Savannakhet. From 2–4 August the battalion performed the last airborne operation of the First Indochina War, jumping into the town of Phanop to link up with militia units and sweep the territory up to the Mu Gia Pass.

Following the Indochina ceasefire on 6 August 1954 the 981-strong BPL was brought back to Seno. After French officers left the unit in October the name of the unit was simplified to 1 Bataillon Parachutiste (1 BP). In 1955 the 1ere Groupement de Commandos Parachutistes Laotiens was integrated with 1 BP at Seno. The battalion conducted a parachute reinforcement jump into Muong Peun during the year.

2 Bataillon Parachutiste

In 1957 a 2 BP began forming at Wattay Airbase. During the following year it was brought up to strength following the return of a contingent trained at the Scout Ranger course in the Philippines. 2 BP was given responsibility for northern operations while 1 BP handled southern missions; both battalions were commanded by majors; a lieutenant-colonel commanded the two-battalion Airborne Regiment.

In May 1959 2 BP was parachuted near Tha Thom, south of the Plain of Jars, to cut off a Communist Pathet Lao battalion fleeing toward the North Vietnamese border. The mission failed to stop the Pathet Lao, and the malaria-ridden 2 BP was withdrawn to Wattay the next month. In July the unit was rushed to Sam Neua after an alleged Pathet Lao/North Vietnamese invasion jeopardized the city. Although most of the government forces had fled from the area, 2 BP found only minimal insurgent activity. On 22 August 1 BP was brought up from Seno to conduct a parachute reinforcement jump into Muong Peun. Both battalions engaged in small skirmishes in northern Laos during September.

In early 1960 2 BP was rushed down to Attopeu to counter increased Pathet Lao activity in the region. The battalion conducted sweeps along the Cambodian border until flown back to Vientiane on 27 April.

To provide additional training for the two para battalions US advisors built a new base 17 km from Vientiane and began providing instruction to a company from 1 BP during February 1960. Elements of 2 BP assembled there in April, but were withdrawn and parachuted north of Vientiane on 2 May in an unsuccessful attempt to apprehend a band of Pathet Lao leaders who had escaped from prison in the capital. Further training was provided at the Royal Thai Army Airborne Ranger base at Lopburi. Companies from 2 BP were rotated through Lopburi in the first half of 1960; nearly the entire 1 BP was sent to Thailand on 6 June. At the same time, a 3 BP had started forming at Wattay.

On 9 August 1960 2 BP, led by its deputy commander

Capt. Kong Le, seized control of Vientiane in order to 'restore neutrality' to Laos. Kong Le was immediately opposed by rightist army officers, who began plotting a counter-revolution from Savannakhet. 1 BP was returned from Lopburi to Seno, and declared its loyalty to the rightists; 3 BP, still four months from graduation, had one company defect to the Kong Le Neutralists; the remainder of the unit refused to support Kong Le and were held hostage at Vientiane.

During September a company of 1 BP was flown to reinforce Sam Neua in the face of pressure from joint Kong Le/Pathet Lao forces. In the same month 2 BP parachuted a team near Mahaxay to harass the rightist forces. During November another contingent from 1 BP was flown to Luang Prabang to reinforce rightist elements. In late November the rightists began their offensive on Vientiane. By 8 December 1 BP had advanced to Paksane. Over the following three days the battalion parachuted east of Vientiane, linking up with 3 BP and other sympathetic army units. 2 BP, supported by Pathet Lao units and North Vietnamese artillery teams, were pushed out of the capital by the third week of December and fled north.

On New Year's Day 1961 the Kong Le/Pathet Lao forces successfully occupied the strategic Plain of Jars. 1 BP jumped onto the southern edge of the plain on 2–3 January 1961 in an attempt to rally government forces, but was forced to withdraw on foot to Tha Thom by 8 January. Over the next month the government attempted several unsuccessful offensives against the Kong Le Neutralists. During this period airborne designations became confused as new para battalions were added to the order-of-battle. The elements of 1 BP occupying Tha Thom were redesignated 11 BP; and 12 BP was raised in Savannakhet in mid-January, with two of its companies flown to Luang Prabang on 17 January. The understrength 3 BP remained at Vientiane.

During February and March 12 BP remained at Luang Prabang, 3 BP operated north of Vientiane, and 11 BP was at Tha Thom. Almost 100 paratroopers from 12 BP were dropped at Tha Thom as reinforcements on 4 February. In addition, a new 55 BP had been raised at Seno, with elements sent to Paksane. On 5 April one company from the reconstituted 1 BP was dropped over Muong Kassy to trap a Neutralist contingent fighting along the Vientiane–Luang Prabang highway; the remainder of the battalion was heli-lifted into the vicinity later that day. After reinforcements failed to arrive, the battalion was forced to evacuate on foot to Luang Prabang on 14 April.

On 24 April all airborne units were gathered under the new regimental-sized Groupement Mobile 15 (Airborne) at Seno. During May, 3 BP and 12 BP were absorbed into 55 BP, leaving only 1, 11, and 55 BP in GM 15. The GM was commanded by a colonel; battalions, each numbering 524 men divided into a headquarters and four companies, were commanded by majors. For the remainder of 1961, GM 15 conducted small-scale sweeps north and east of Savannakhet.

On 12 February 1962, 1 BP was withdrawn from its static defence positions east of Savannakhet and parachuted into the north-western town of Nam Tha. As enemy pressure built up around Nam Tha, 55 BP was dropped in on 27 March, and 11 BP on 16 April. After weeks of heavy enemy pressure during April, 1 BP began advancing toward the nearby enemy-held town of Muong Sing on 3 May. The battalion was smashed, sending the paratroopers fleeing back to Nam Tha and precipitating a mass exodus toward the Thai border.

Only 55 BP offered any resistance, losing half its strength in the process. GM 15 was not reconstituted at Seno until 25 May. The paratroopers spent the rest of 1962 replacing their losses.

In early 1963, 55 BP, recognized as the best unit in GM 15, was sent on small-scale clearing operations in Military Region 4 (Pakse). During November, 11 BP advanced toward the North Vietnamese border, clearing the Pathet Lao from the town of Lak Sao. Though they were initially successful, a strong North Vietnamese counter-attack in December put 11 BP in danger of being destroyed; 55 BP was parachuted east of Lak Sao to provide cover as 11 BP successfully withdrew toward the Mekong.

In April 1964 three para battalions of the paramilitary Directorate of National Co-ordination (DNC) took over Vientiane in a coup d'état. The DNC had its origins in September 1960, when a Groupement Mobile Speciale (GMS) composed of 11 and 33 Bataillons Speciales (BS) was raised under the command of Lt. Col. Siho Lamphouthacoul. The GMS was used during the retaking of Vientiane from Kong Le, capturing Wattay Airbase on 16 December. In March 1961 the GMS was combined with intelligence, psychological warfare, military police, and national police units to form the DNC. During the following year a 30-man contingent was sent to Hua Hin, Thailand, to receive commando and airborne training. Upon their return they formed the cadre of the new 99 BS, the third battalion in the GMS. A DNC airborne course was established at Pon Kheng in Vientiane and 11, 33, and 99 BS were all given parachute

PASKHAS jumpmasters. Note Air Force Special Forces qualification badge over left pocket on right figure.

training. Elements of these three parachute battalions were stationed at Phou Khao Khouai, north of Vientiane.

In early 1964 the GMS was brought down to Savannakhet to capture the town of Nong Boua Lao. Before the three para battalions could reach their objective they were withdrawn in April to conduct the coup d'état in Vientiane. Although rated as the most capable military unit in Laos, the GMS was primarily kept in Vientiane to support the illicit activities of certain corrupt officials.

In May 1964 Kong Le's Neutralist Forces were attacked on the Plain of Jars by their former allies, the Communist Pathet Lao. The original 2 BP, which had swelled to six companies while it was defending Vientiane in late 1960, had been sub-divided, with each of the first five companies becoming a separate Neutralist BP and the sixth company becoming an Airborne Training Centre at Muang Phanh. Because of the lack of aircraft, few of the Neutralist paratroopers were airborne qualified. Four of the para battalions—1, 2, 3, and 4 BP—were stationed on the Plain of Jars; 5 BP had been sent to the central Laotian town of Nhommarath in 1962, but had been pulled back after clashes with the Pathet Lao in June 1963.

When the Pathet Lao launched a major offensive against Kong Le in May 1964, 1 and 4 BP defected to the Communists. The remaining forces pulled back west of the Plain of Jars; the Airborne Training Centre was moved to Vang Vieng.

In November 1964 GM 15 launched Operation 'Victorious Arrow', a clearing operation east of Savannakhet. During the following year elements of each GM 15 para battalion were brought to Lopburi for recon and commando training.

PASKHAS HALO parachutists with folding-stock FNC rifles.

The overthrow of the DNC

On 1 February 1965 the DNC, which had held *de facto* control over Vientiane during the previous year, was defeated in yet another coup d'état. The GMS, which had been renamed Border Police in August 1964, remained at Phou Khao Khouai and refused to surrender. After two days of negoti-ations, however, the GMS agreed to lay down their arms with the option of transferring to the regular armed forces. By mid-year they had been moved to Seno to form the core of a new parachute regiment, GM 21 (Airborne), composed of 33, 66, and 99 BP.

GM 21 quickly became the best regiment in the Laotian army. In November 1965 it was rushed to Thakhek after two NVA battalions came close to overrunning the town. Com-mand of the regiment was held by Col. Thao Ly, previously the commander of the three GMS para battalions.

In October 1966 Kong Le went into exile and his Neutralist Armed Forces were organized into Groupements Mobiles. GM 801, located at Muong Soui, was composed of the newly-formed 85 BP and two regular battalions; GM 802 was formed at Pakse out of 2, 5, and a reconstituted 4 BP. The airborne-qualified 1 Bataillon Commando Speciale, which had been trained in Indonesia in 1965, was disbanded and its members dispersed to the other para battalions.

During 1967 GM 15 remained in static defence positions around Muong Phalane. One of its battalions, 55 BP, was briefly sent to the extreme north-western corner of the country to confront warring opium smugglers. GM 21 rotated two of its battalions to Military Region 4 for operations around Khong Sedone, Saravane, and Lao Ngam. The Airborne Training Centre at Seno, advised by members of the French military mission, was commanded by a major.

In the opening days of January 1968 the entire GM 15 was rushed to the northern garrison of Nam Bac to counter heavy NVA pressure. On 8 January, with pressure nearing the breaking point, 99 BP was landed north of the garrison. Nam Bac fell the following day, resulting in the total destruction of 99 BP and the near disintegration of GM 15.

In August, all Groupements Mobiles in the Laotian Army were abolished, replaced by independent battalions. The two battalions of GM 21 and the remnants of GM 15 were consolidated into the independent 101, 102, and 103 BP. All three, plus the Airborne Training Centre, were based at Seno.

The Neutralist Groupements Mobiles were not disbanded until the following year after GM 801 was crushed at Muong Soui and brought to Thailand for retraining. The para elements in GM 801 were grouped into the new Bataillon Commando 208, and sent to Vang Vieng. From GM 802, 5 BP was converted into 104 BP, and the other airborne elements were gathered into Bataillon Commando 207; both of these battalions were stationed in Pakse.

During 1969 the three airborne battalions of the Lao army were shuttled across the country in reinforcement operations. In January all three launched successful attacks east of Savannakhet into North Vietnamese-held territory. One battalion was then heli-lifted into Thateng in Military Region 4 on 4 April. BP 103 was sent to northern Laos in May to help government forces briefly capture the Communist-held town of Xieng Khouangville. In September BP 101 replaced BP 103 in the north and was used in an unsuccessful attempt to recapture the town of Muong Soui.

During the same year, three companies totalling 340 men completed airborne and ranger training at Lopburi. Based at

Ban Y Lai, north of Vientiane, the unit was known as the Military Region 5 Commandos (MR 5 Cdos.) and was used primarily on counter-insurgency sweeps around Vientiane. In later years the MR 5 Cdos. were used in other military regions to demonstrate symbolic support from the Vientiane government: during September 1971 two companies participated in Operation 'Golden Mountain', the successful capture of Phou Khout; in 1972 two companies were sent to Military Region 4 to help in the recapture of Khong Sedone. As late as May 1975 a single remaining company from the MR 5 Cdos. was fighting north of the capital.

In 1970, BP 101 was sent to Luang Prabang to halt a North Vietnamese advance toward the city. During the final month of the year a para battalion was sent to reinforce a guerrilla staging base, PS 22, on the eastern rim of the Bolovens Plateau.

In mid-1971, following the fall of the southern city of Paksong to the NVA, the Neutralist BP 104 and BC 207 were used during a prolonged government counter-offensive. Also used was the Laotian Army's 7th Infantry Battalion based at Pakse, which had been allowed to send some of its men through airborne training because its commander was the brother of the Military Region commander. In late 1971 planning began for the consolidation of all infantry battalions into two light divisions: the 1st Division based at Vientiane and the 2nd Strike Division at Seno. Both divisions, each composed of three light brigades, were formally created on 23 March 1972. The three independent airborne battalions—BP 101, 102, and 103—were dissolved and integrated into among the 2nd Strike Division's 22 Brigade.

SPECOM

Construction began in late 1971 on a training centre at Seno to provide commando instruction for the 2nd Strike Division. The training cadre, consisting of several graduates of US Army Special Forces training in the US, were converted during 1972 into the core of an elite SPECOM, short for Special Commando, directly under the commanding officer of the 2nd Strike Division. By mid-1972 SPECOM had two airborne reconnaissance companies, each broken into 12-man recon teams. A third recon company, composed of 140 former members of the airborne-qualified Savannakhet Commando Raider Teams (see MAA 217 *The War in Laos 1960–75*), and a Heavy Weapons company were transferred to SPECOM in mid-1973.

Indonesian Special Forces qualification badges: Pathfinder (left); HALO (right).

SPECOM was first used in late 1972 to secure an H-34 helicopter crash site north-east of Seno. In the opening months of 1973 SPECOM recon teams were sent to Thakhek when NVA forces began pressuring the city. By mid-year SPECOM was heli-lifted north-east of Seno to place a listening station on Phou Sang He Mountain near the Ho Chi Minh Trail. A planned SPECOM assault into Vientiane after renegade Air Force officers captured Wattay Airfield in August was cancelled when the coup attempt quickly fell apart.

In April 1974 SPECOM's 2 Co. was moved to Vientiane to provide VIP security for rightist members of the new coalition government. In May elements of the 2nd Strike Divisions's three under-strength brigades were converted into three para battalions—711, 712, and 713 BP—under the new 7 Para Brigade at Seno. SPECOM, which numbered 412 men, was converted into the brigade's fourth para battalion, 714 BP.

In early 1975 elements of 714 BP were brought to Thakhek in an unsuccessful attempt to quell pro-Communist demonstrations. By May the 7 Para Brigade was disbanded after Pathet Lao forces took control of Vientiane.

Indonesia: Marine Special Forces

In 1960 a cadre of Indonesian Marines received training at the British-run Jungle Warfare Centre in Malaya. During the following year a second group attended US Marine reconnaissance training at Coranado. These cadres were combined to form the core of an élite reconnaissance unit combining airborne and amphibious skills. Officially created on 18 March 1961, the unit was called *Komando Intai Para Amphibi* (KIPAM, or Amphibious Recon Para-Commando).

Set at company strength, KIPAM was first used in the reconnaissance role during the Irian Jaya operation in April 1962. It was next used during the Confrontation with Malaysia, conducting coastal reconnaissance operations along the Malay peninsula. During the December 1974 East Timor operation, KIPAM was again used in the reconnaissance role. In 1971 KIPAM was expanded on paper to a 976-man battalion; actual strength, however, remained at only 300 throughout the 1980s. One detachment is stationed in Jakarta; the remainder are garrisoned at the KIPAM training centre in Surabaya.

KIPAM accepts volunteers from the Marines with at least two years' experience. Seven months of commando training include a one-month airborne course: airborne qualification wings are presented after five day jumps, one night jump, and one 'rough terrain' jungle jump. Refresher jumps are conducted into the water. The standard parachute is the US T-10.

The standard KIPAM recon team consists of nine men. Equipment is normal Marine issue, an exception being the choice of assault rifle: rather than the M-16 of the Marine Corps, KIPAM uses both the licence-built Belgian FNC and the durable Soviet AK-47. Select KIPAM members have benefited over the years from overseas training with the US Marine Force Recon, US Navy UDT/SEALs, US Army Rangers, and British Marine Commandos. In 1979 a joint

Indonesian KOPASSANDHA in training, 1983.

exercise was held between KIPAM, Indonesian UDT detachments and US Navy SEALs.

To provide an underwater demolitions and salvage capability, the Indonesian Navy created an Underwater Demolitions Team in 1962. Called PASKA, the unit is stationed in Surabaya and is not airborne-qualified. PASKA trained the initial Malaysian PASKAL cadre.

Air Force Special Forces

The Indonesian Air Force paratroopers are the oldest airborne formation in the country. During the anti-Dutch revolution a guerrilla cadre was formed within the fledgling air force; and on 17 October 1949 nine men from this group were parachuted into Kalimantan to incite an anti-colonial uprising. This date is celebrated as the founding day of the Indonesian Air Force paratroopers.

During the early 1950s the initial Air Force guerrilla cadre was expanded into the *Pasukan Pertahanan Pangkalan* (PPP), or Air Base Defence Force. Drawing from PPP members, an airborne-qualified *Pasukan Gerak Tjepat* (PGT), or Quick

Mobile Force, was raised by the mid-1950s. The PGT was soon thrown into action in West Java during the DI/TII Islamic rebellion. In 1958 PGT detachments were parachuted north of Sulawesi to act as a shock force during the Permesta rebellion, and into Sumatra during the same year to retake key cities from mutinous army units. In 1962, elements jumped into Sorong and Fak Fak during the 'Trikora Operation to liberate Irian Jaya.

In mid-1964 the PGT saw extensive action during the Confrontation with Malaysia. On 17 August members of the force infiltrated by small boat south-west of Johore on the Malay peninsula in an attempt to organize anti-Malaysian rebels. Two weeks later over 100 PGT paras jumped at night near Labis in north Johore. Several further seaborne infiltrations were conducted during the final months of the year.

By 1965 the PGT totalled three para battalions with a headquarters at Bandung. In the wake of the September Communist coup attempt it was renamed the *Komando Pasukan Gerak Chepat* (KOPASGAT), or Quick Mobile Commando Force. KOPASGAT consisted of one Command Headquarters in Bandung and three Quick Mobile Force Wings in Jakarta, Bandung, and Surabaya totalling 3,000 men in ten Assault Battalions (Airborne). Its primary mission was airborne special operations. Elements of the force jumped into East Timor in December 1975 to secure the airfield.

In 1983 KOPASGAT was renamed *Pasukan Khusus TNI-AU* (PASKHAS), or Air Force Special Forces. Its mission was limited to airbase security, seizing airfields, search and rescue, pathfinding, and providing forward air guides. In 1989

PASKHAS was commanded by an Air Force air marshal and composed of one Command Headquarters in Bandung and six airborne Special Forces Squadrons numbered 461 to 466. Detachments are stationed at airbases across the country, and one company is kept on the disputed Natuna Island. A PASKHAS Training Depot Squadron is kept at its Bandung headquarters; airborne and commando courses are held at Margahayu, near Bandung. Seven jumps must be completed for parachute qualification.

Army Special Forces

On 16 April 1952 preparations began for the formation of a commando unit to be assigned to the élite Siliwangi Division. Training was conducted at Batujajar near the east Javan city of Bandung. One year later the commando unit was removed from the Siliwangi Division and put under the command of Army Headquarters. Over the next two years this small élite cadre was known as the *Korps Komando Angatan Darat* (KKAD), or Army Commando Corps; In 1955 it was renamed the *Regimen Pasukan Komando Angatan Darat* (RPKAD), or Army Commando Regiment.

During the following year the RPKAD became embroiled in domestic politics after its Sudanese commander lent his support to conspirators within the Armed Forces. In November he moved the commandos from Batujajar to the outskirts of Jakarta in anticipation of a coup d'état. No reinforcements arrived, however, and the unit moved back to Batujajar. A mutiny among NCOs within the regiment later that month gave the Army Headquarters an excuse to arrest the commander and bring the RPKAD firmly back under government control.

In early 1958 anti-Javan discontent, led by rebel Sumatran army units, was fast spreading across the island of Sumatra. Spearheading the government counter-offensive, 600 RPKAD commandos parachuted into central Sumatra on the morning of 12 March, capturing the city of Pakanbaru and eventually putting down the rebellion. On 26 October 1959, the RPKAD was renamed the *Regimen Para-Komando Angatan Darat* (RPKAD), or Army Para-Commando Regiment.

In 1962 the RPKAD was in the forefront of the next major operation, the retaking of Dutch-held West Irian (now called Irian Jaya). On 4 May a company from the regiment's single battalion was dropped from C-47 aircraft near the coastal city of Fak Fak; four more planeloads of commandos were dropped in the same vicinity on 15 May. Almost a dozen other jumps were conducted in late May and June near Fak Fak, Merauke, and Kaimana. While much of their time was spent evading Dutch patrols, the Irian Jaya operation increased confidence within the RPKAD.

Following the Irian Jaya operation the RPKAD was expanded to three 600-man battalions: 1 Para-Cdo. Bn. in Jakarta, 2 Para-Cdo. Bn. in Ambon in the Maluku Islands, and 3 Para-Cdo. Bn. in Solo, central Java. In October 1963 elements of these battalions began to train Malaysian insurgents being sent into Sabah during the Confrontation. The RPKAD also participated itself in cross-border operations against British Commonwealth forces in Malaysia until late 1964.

In mid-1965 leftist army officers began conspiring with members of the Communist Party of Indonesia to stage a coup d'état in Jakarta. When the coup materialized during the first week of October the staunchly anti-Communist 1 Para-Cdo. Bn., which had resisted attempts by the conspirators to be dispatched to Kalimantan, joined 2 Para-Cdo. Bn., which had just arrived from Solo to participate in a 5 October Jakarta parade, to confront the Communist rebels. Both battalions were quickly tasked with seizing Halim Airbase outside the capital from rebel forces, which they did on 2 October. 1 Para-Cdo. Bn. then retook the radio station. After it became clear that Communist resistance inside Jakarta was crumbling the RPKAD was sent to central Java to crush rebels in Semerang and Solo. On 22 November the regiment scored a major victory when it captured the leader of the Communist Party of Indonesia. During the following month it was sent to the island of Bali to control anti-leftist riots that were sweeping the nation.

By early 1967 the RPKAD was in the forefront of rightist forces poised to take full control in Jakarta. On 11 March three RPKAD companies in civilian clothes approached the palace of President Sukarno. The intimidated president quickly fled the capital and soon resigned his presidency. Over the next five months the regiment participated in the arrest of several leftist ministers, and helped purge disloyal army officers across central Java. Once stability had returned to Indonesia by the year's end the RPKAD was one of the most politically powerful units in the country. To bolster its capabilities the regiment added two special warfare groups, each composed of three battalion-sized *karsayud*; 1 Group was stationed in Jakarta, 2 Group in Solo.

KOPASSANDHA

On 17 February 1971 the RPKAD was renamed the *Komando Pasukan Sandhi Yudha* (KOPASSANDHA), or Unconventional Warfare Force. Commanded by a major general, KOPASSANDHA was divided into four groups plus the Batujajar Training Centre. 1 and 3 Groups held a para-commando mission; each was composed of 1,800 men divided into three battalion-sized 'Combat Detachments'. 1 Group, which traced its lineage back to the RPKAD's original three

Indonesian Special Forces shoulder insignia worn by the RPKAD and KOPASSANDHA (left), and KOPASSUS (right).

KOPASSANDHA member dressed in Special Forces camouflage. The SF beret badge is pinned on the jungle hat; cloth SF qualification badge, Army wings, and marksman badge are above the left pocket.

RPKAD Para-Commando battalions, was stationed initially in Jakarta, then shifted in 1980 to Serang, West Java. 3 Group, brought to full strength in 1980, was originally stationed in Solo, then moved to Ujung Pandang, south Sulawesi.

The second half of KOPASSANDHA was composed of two *Sandhi Yudha*, or Special Warfare, groups: 2 Group was stationed in Jakarta, 4 Group in Solo. These 600-man groups, successors of the two RPKAD special warfare groups, operated in a true special forces/unconventional warfare role.

KOPASSANDHA was placed administratively under the Army chief-of-staff; operationally, it came directly under the head of the Department of Defence and Security. As an élite reserve it took over many of the responsibilities previously held by the Army's KOSTRAD Strategic Reserve.

In 1974 KOPASSANDHA was called upon to train Timorese nationalists to counter the rise of Timorese rebels in the Portuguese colony of East Timor. Over the next year the situation in East Timor grew worse after the FRETILIN nationalist group declared independence in the wake of a Portuguese withdrawal. Advance KOPASSANDHA units moved into the border village of Batugade in October and started staging cross-border forays into Timor. After FRETILIN forces continued to consolidate their hold, Jakarta began to plan Operasi Seroja (Operation 'Lotus'), the invasion of East Timor. During the pre-dawn hours of 7

December 1975 commandos from KOPASSANDHA's 1 Group boarded C-130 aircraft at Jogjakarta; at 0600, they jumped into the East Timor capital of Dili, securing areas of the city for subsequent jumps by KOSTRAD airborne infantry.

KOPASSANDHA distinguished itself during the opening phases, spearheading the capture of key towns. To counter FRETILIN insurgent activity in the countryside KOPASSANDHA was used in late 1978 as a heliborne strike force across East Timor. On the last day of that year KOPASSANDHA was able to locate and kill the movement's president.

In 1982 KOPASSANDHA continued to operate in East Timor, this time providing instructors for the training of local forces. During August 1983 KOPASSANDHA was used against FRETILIN during Operasi Sapu Bersih (Operation 'Clean Sweep'). In late 1983 KOPASSANDHA forces were employed against the Free Papua Movement, a guerrilla group seeking the independence of Irian Jaya. Additional KOPASSANDHA commandos were brought into Irian Jaya during February 1984.

KOPASSUS

In 1985 KOPASSANDHA was renamed *Komando Pasukan Khussus* (KOPASSUS), or Special Commando Force. A deliberate effort was made to streamline the special forces, focusing on quality instead of quantity. In 1989 the 2,500-man KOPASSUS consisted of 1 Group, composed of 11 and 12 Battalions, stationed in Jakarta; and 2 Group, composed of 21 and 22 Battalions, in Solo, central Java. The former KOPASSANDHA 3 Group was removed from Special Forces command and transferred to the Army KOSTRAD Strategic Reserve; the KOPASSUS 3 Group now refers to the training unit at Batujajar. KOPASSUS command is held by a brigadier-general; groups are commanded by colonels.

Indonesian Special Forces are additionally tasked with anti-terrorist and anti-hijack operations. Their first experience in counter-terrorism came in March 1981, when Indonesian Islamic extremists hijacked a DC-9 in Jakarta with 55 hostages aboard. On 28 March the plane landed in Bangkok and the hijackers demanded money and the release of their colleagues from Indonesian jails. During the following day negotiators and 36 commandos from KOPASSANDHA's 1 and 4 Groups flew to Bangkok. During the evening of 30 March the Indonesian government stalled for time by announcing that it would bow to the demands of the hijackers. At 0240 hours the following morning the commandos approached the aircraft from the rear in single file. Throwing ladders on the wings, they quickly blew open the doors. A terrorist appeared at the front door and was shot dead; three of the four remaining hijackers were similarly dispatched. All hostages were freed, with only one member of the assault force and the chief pilot being wounded. The entire operation lasted three minutes.

To better deal with counter-terrorist contingencies, Detachment 81 was created in late 1981. Commanded by a lieutenant-colonel fresh from training with West Germany's GSG 9, Detachment 81 falls administratively under Special Forces headquarters. Teams from the detachment have been rotated through East Timor to give them experience against insurgent forces.

Since 1962 the Special Forces also contain scuba-trained elements. Initially trained at the Navy UDT course, the

Indonesian SF insignia: beret badge (top left); chest qualification badge (top right); KOPASSANDHA and KOPASSUS 1 Group shoulder tab (bottom left); KOPASSANDHA and KOPASSUS Headquarters shoulder tab, also worn by Detachment 81 members (bottom right).

Special Forces established their own school at Batujajar in 1967. At present both of the KOPASSUS combat groups have 80-man scuba detachments.

Special Forces training has traditionally been extensive. Volunteers are accepted after completing two years of light infantry training. A seven-month SF course at Batujajar follows, ending with a five-week airborne course. Parachute wings are awarded after five day, one night, and one jungle jump. Additional qualifications are offered to Special Forces graduates, such as scuba, HALO, jumpmaster, and a two-and-a-half-month pathfinder course.

The tough reputation of Batu Jajar has attracted foreign students. In 1965 Laos sent 150 pupils for commando training, and in 1972 the Khmer Republic sent 60 students. Malaysians regularly attend the school. Most recently, a contingent of Bangladeshi trainees graduated from basic commando training in 1987; a second Bangladeshi 30-man group arrived in 1988 for a jumpmaster course.

Army Airborne Infantry

By 1961 the best units of the three Java-based infantry divisions became airborne-qualified to give the government a quick response capability. These included 328 and 330 Para-Raider Battalions, both from the Kujang Regiment of the Siliwongi Division; 530 Para Battalion of the Brawidaja Division in east Java; and 454 Para Battalion of the Diponegoro Division in central Java. Elements of 330 Para-Raider Battalion were sent in 1963 to the Congo to perform UN peace-keeping duties.

During the Communist coup attempt of 1966 airborne infantry played a significant role during fighting within the capital. 454 Para Bn. and 530 Para Bn., each numbering 1,000 men, were brought into Jakarta and sided with the Communists. Also loyal to the leftists was the Cakrabirawa Palace Guard, a three-battalion airborne regiment charged with protecting President Sukarno.

Aligned against the Communists in Jakarta was 328 Para-Raider Bn.; in addition, 530 Para Bn. soon purged itself of Communist elements and switched its loyalty over to the rightists.

Following the failed coup attempt, the Cakrabirawa Guard was disbanded in mid-April 1967 after Sukarno fled the capital. Other airborne units were raised around the country, including 100 Para Bn. in Medan, 531 Para Bn. in east Java, 600 Para Bn. in Kalimantan, and 700 Para Bn. in Ujang Pandang, south Sulawesi. In addition, the airborne Kujang Regt. of the Siliwongi Division was augmented in 1967 by 305 Para Bn., which was immediately sent on operations in west Kalimantan.

KOPASSANDHA 3 Group, 1983, armed with the French LRAC 89 anti-tank weapon and folding-stock FNC.

In 1967 the Army's KOSTRAD Strategic Reserve was expanded from a cavalry formation to include amphibious and airborne capabilities. As a result, 430, 454, and 530 Para Bns. were transferred into KOSTRAD. By the early 1970s the KOSTRAD included 17 and 18 Para Brigades, located in western and eastern Java respectively. 18 Bde. jumped into Dili during the December 1971 East Timor operation.

Following major reorganization of the Indonesian Armed Forces in early 1986 KOSTRAD was divided into two divisions. Within the 1st Division is the three-battalion 17 Para Bde.; 18 Para Bde. is part of the 2nd Division. In addition, KOSTRAD assumed control over 3 Para-Cdo. Bde. at Ujang Pandang, formerly the KOPASSANDHA 3 Group.

All KOSTRAD airborne training is conducted at KOPASSUS facilities at Batujajar.

Police Mobile Brigade

The Mobile Brigade, which began forming in late 1946 and was used during the anti-Dutch Revolution, started sending students for US Army SF training on Okinawa in January 1959. In April 1960 a second contingent arrived for two months of ranger training. By the mid-1960s the three-battalion Mobile Brigade, commonly known as Brimob, had been converted into an élite shock force. A Brimob airborne training centre was established at Bandung.

Following the 1965 coup attempt one Brimob battalion was used during anti-Communist operations in west Kalimantan.

In December 1975 a Brimob battalion was used during the East Timor operation. During the late 1970s Brimob assumed VIP security and urban anti-terrorist duties. After the formation of Detachment 81, counter-terrorist responsibilities were removed from the Mobile Brigade. In 1989 Brimob still contained airborne-qualified elements. *Pelopor* ('Ranger') and airborne training takes place in Bandung and at a training camp outside Jakarta.

Indonesian KOSTRAD insignia: unit shoulder insignia and tab (left); beret badge (right).

Malaysia:
Army Special Forces

On 2 March 1965 the Royal Malaysian Army raised on paper an élite unit for 'special duty'; called the Malaysian Special Service Unit, its strength was set at ten officers and 296 men. Initial selection was made at Sungai Besi in Kuala Lumpur; training was then shifted to Majidee Camp in Johore Baharu. Assistance was provided by the British 40th Royal Marine Commando, upon which the Malaysians consciously patterned the unit. Once training was completed the unit was posted to Sebatang Kra near Port Diction. Additional trainees were sent to Indonesia in 1968.

In August 1970 the Special Service Unit was renamed the Malaysian Special Service Regiment (MSSR); kept at battalion strength, the regiment was moved from Sebatang Kra to Sungai Udang, Melaka. Aircraft were posted at the new site and used to airborne-qualify MSSR members. In 1977 a second regiment, 2 MSSR, was raised and stationed at Sungai Udang.

A major reorganization took place in 1981, with 1 and 2 MSSR being renamed 65 and 70 Commando for a few months; the names were soon changed, with the original 1 and 2 MSSR redesignated 21 and 22 Para Commando respectively. Both of these battalion-sized formations specialize in raiding and amphibious missions. Each regiment has 45

officers and 1,140 men and is composed of a headquarters staff, Administrative Squadron, Support Squadron (Mortar Troop, Signal Troop, Boat Troop, and Reinforcement Troop), Training Squadron, and four Assault Squadrons. Each Assault Squadron has 155 men divided into one Heavy Weapons Troop and four Assault Troops. Assault Troops (one officer, 35 men) are further divided into ten-man operational sections.

Two more battalions, 11 and 12 Special Service Regts., were raised in 1981 with an unconventional warfare orientation. Authorized strength for each includes a headquarters staff, Administrative Squadron, Support Squadron, and four Reconnaissance Squadrons. Reconnaissance squadrons are broken into four recon troops of one officer and 19 men each; troops are then split into five-man recon sections (section commander, section deputy, scout, signaller, and engineer). Because of budgetary limitations 12 Special Service Regt. reached a strength of only two reconnaissance squadrons before its manpower was dispersed to the three other special forces regiments. Currently, only a skeleton headquarters detachment for 12 Special Service Regt. is maintained.

In 1981 all four army SF regiments were gathered under the Malaysian Special Service Group (MSSG). MSSG headquarters is in Kuala Lumpur; all regimental headquarters are at Sungai Udang. Command of the MSSG is held by a Brigadier; regiments are headed by lieutenant-colonels.

KOSTRAD paratrooper, 1983; he wears the KOSTRAD unit insignia and tab on the left shoulder.

In addition to the MSSG, the Malaysian Ministry of Defence announced in 1986 that it would convert an infantry battalion into an airborne infantry battalion. The unit converted was 8 Ranger Battalion of the Royal Malaysian Ranger Regt., now stationed at Terendak Camp, Melaka. The Ministry of Defence has also announced plans to airborne-qualify two more battalions by the turn of the century.

In 1976, a new Special Warfare Training Centre was opened at Sungai Udang, and now conducts all SF and airborne courses for the MSSG. These facilities, which contain airborne and scuba courses, are considered among the best in South-East Asia. Basic special warfare training lasts 12 weeks. After completion, students receive airborne training and carry out eight parachute jumps, including one night and one jungle jump. MSSG students have also co-trained with US, British, Australian and New Zealand SF units.

The Malaysian Army SF are disciplined and well trained. Like many other élite units, they will be used in an independent tactical role during hostilities. Though they have not been tested against a foreign aggressor, the Malaysian SF have proved their skills during extended combat experience against Malaysia's own Communist insurgents.

Air Force Special Forces
In 1978 the Royal Malaysian Air Force began forming the HANDAU (*Pertahanan Udara*, or 'Air Force Ground Defence Unit'), an airborne-qualified squadron tasked with airbase security and jungle rescue operations. HANDAU Regimental

Headquarters is in Kuala Lumpur, with detachments at most major airbases; command is held by a lieutenant colonel. The initial HANDAU cadre was trained by the Army SF at Sungai Udang and posted to Sungai Besi in Kuala Lumpur. Until 1986 HANDAU airborne training was conducted by the Army; HANDAU now conducts its own parachute and commando courses. Some HANDAU personnel have been trained in Australia, Indonesia, and the US.

HANDAU has not been used in combat. A jungle rescue team from the force was used in January 1982 to rappel into the jungle 20 miles north-east of Kuala Lumpur to rescue the Malaysian Foreign Minister from an air crash. HANDAU teams have also rescued downed Air Force pilots.

Navy Special Forces
The Royal Malaysian Navy formed its own commando unit, the PASKAL (*Pasukan Khas Laut*, or 'Special Sea Unit'), in 1983. The original cadre was trained by PASKA, the Indonesian Combat Diver unit. Apart from airborne training conducted by the Army SF, PASKAL now conducts its own commando courses. During the early 1980s PASKAL participated in joint exercises with US Navy SEALs. In 1988 the unit took on additional responsibilities for anti-piracy and hostage-rescue operations at sea. The battalion-sized formation is led by a navy commander and headquartered at Lumut

An airborne-qualified KOSTRAD officer talks with troops dressed in distinctive vertical-striped KOSTRAD camouflage.

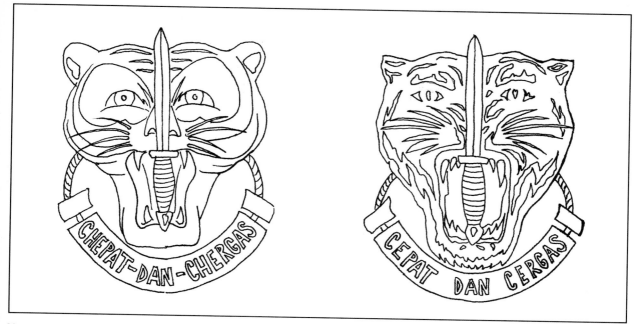

Navy Base, Perak. Apart from limited operations in eastern Malaysia, PASKAL has not been used in combat operations.

Malaysian Special Service beret badges: old-style (left), and current issue (right). Note change in spelling to conform with new Malay grammatical rules.

Police Commandos

On 25 October 1969 the Malaysian Police Field Force began forming a special commando unit modelled on the British Special Air Service. Known as 'Vat 69', the unit received initial airborne training in Thailand and commando training from the British. Vat 69 is currently at battalion strength, including a freefall team. It is headquartered in Kuala Lumpur and led by a lieutenant-colonel. As part of the Police Field Force, Vat 69 is responsible for special counter-insurgency operations, and is Malaysia's main anti-terrorist and hostage rescue force. The unit works closely with police field intelligence operatives from the Special Branch. Like the British SAS, Vat 69 commandos wear a sand-coloured beret. The beret badge is the standard Police Field Force design on a black backing.

THE PHILIPPINES: SCOUT RANGERS

Immediately after World War Two the newly independent government of the Philippines was threatened in central Luzon province by the Communist-inspired Hukbalahap (Huk) peasant rebellion. As part of the government's counter-insurgency effort Philippine Army Capt. Raphael 'Rocky' Ileto, a West Point graduate and former member of the US 6th Army's famous Alamo Scouts, proposed the creation of an élite army unit to train volunteers in ranger, jungle warfare, commando, and reconnaissance techniques. Because Ileto envisioned combining the deep-penetration reconnaissance

MSSG soldier with CAR-15 rifle.

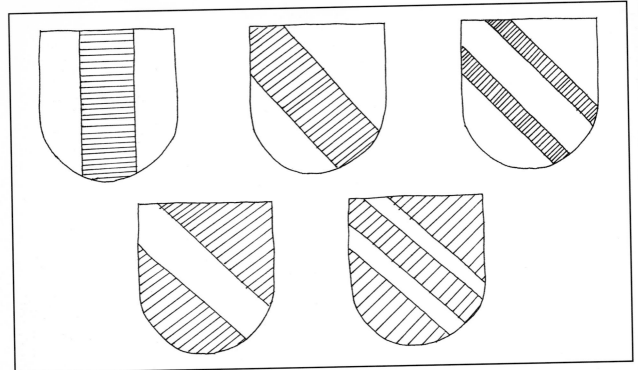

Malaysian Special Service beret flashes: (top row) Special Warfare Training Centre, 21 Para-Commando, 22 Para-Commando; (bottom row) 11 SSR, 12 SSR.

skills of the Alamo Scouts with the quick-strike capability of the US Army's World War Two Ranger Battalions, the name Scout Rangers was chosen. On 25 November 1950 Ileto's Scout Ranger Training Unit was formed.

Intensive Scout Ranger training at Fort McKinley, Manila, produced teams of one officer and four men which were assigned to regular infantry battalions, but usually operated independently in remote areas for extended periods, collecting intelligence and, often, neutralizing targeted Huk leaders. In order to consolidate Scout Ranger graduates into one compact unit, 1 Scout Ranger Regiment (SRR) was activated in 1954. Consisting of one battalion and four independent companies, the SRR was heavily involved in anti-Huk operations during the mid-1950s, performed 1955 election security duties in the troubled province of Leyte, and fought Muslim rebels in the Jolo and Lanao campaigns. In 1957 the SRR was dissolved after the major insurgent threat was neutralized.

During the same year the SRTU was disbanded after graduating Class 13. Immediately prior to its disbandment the SRTU had briefly instituted parachute training at Fort McKinley, ranking the Scout Ranger course as one of the best in South-East Asia. An Advanced Ranger Training Course was continued by a Mobile Training Team within the Army School Center.

On 21 August 1971 President Marcos declared the Philippines threatened by a Communist rebellion and imposed martial law the following month. In response to this threat the SRTU was re-established on 8 December 1971 and resumed training Class 14 after a 14-year hiatus. The SRTU, however,

temporarily lost its independent status after it became organic to the Army Training Center on 1 July 1974. Scout Ranger graduates were assigned to infantry formations and used on counter-insurgency sweeps against Communist rebels in the northern provinces. Rangers also participated in heavy combat against Muslim secessionists in the southern province of Mindinao during the mid-1970s.

On 16 July 1978 the SRTU was removed from the Training Center and expanded into a Scout Ranger Group (SRG) of five independent companies. Commanded by a colonel, the SRG was assigned to the Army's new Special Warfare Brigade. Unlike the earlier Scout Ranger teams, however, the new SRG now looked more like a conventional combat formation than an unconventional reconnaissance unit. Scout Ranger training, which included airmobile doctrine, reflected this change. In addition, select members were given airborne training. The SRG training component meanwhile broadened its mission to include courses in Special Operations, Basic Ranger tactics, Scout Ranger Orientation, and Platoon Leader's Training.

The SRG remained part of the Special Warfare Brigade until the latter's disbandment on 16 March 1983. On the following day the Group was expanded into the newly reactivated 1 Scout Ranger Regiment (SRR) composed initially of two battalions, each with three companies, and an additional nine independent companies. Command of the regiment went to Brig. Gen. Felix Brawner, with regimental headquarters at Fort Bonifacio in Manila. A third battalion, the Scout Ranger Mountain Battalion, began forming the following year and was immediately sent on operations in southern Mindinao. Further expansion of the SRR was planned in early February 1986, to include a fourth battalion and the development of Fort Capinpin outside Manila as a training base for guerrilla warfare.

Scout Rangers after Marcos

The February 1986 Revolution threw the SRR into Manila's political battles. The regiment was initially ordered on 21 February to surround on opposition radio station and, on the following day, to assault the anti-Marcos rebel headquarters in Manila's Camp Crame. On the evening of 23 February two Scout Ranger battalions began to mass for attack, but the troops refused to comply with orders. On the morning of 25 February the SRR announced their loyalty to the anti-Marcos rebels, and led a successful assault on the three remaining pro-Marcos broadcasting transmitters.

With the accession to power of the Aquino government the SRR returned to fighting the Communist New People's Army guerrillas in the countryside. During the closing months of 1986 elements of the regiment engaged the NPA around Davao, where they formed a rapid insertion unit called Task Force Panther.

On 1 December 1986 the SRR was restructured into a National Maneuver Unit. Numbering 2,500 men, the regiment consisted of four battalions (including one Scout Ranger Mountain Battalion) and ten self-sustaining companies. Battalions consisted of three companies totalling 500 men; independent companies ranged from 80 to 100 men. As a National Maneuver Unit, the regiment was now eligible to be sent on operations anywhere in the Philippines; previously, SRR elements tended to remain assigned to one geographic location. The regiment was given priority for transport aircraft, helicopters, special equipment, and intelligence support. At the time of conversion to a National Maneuver Unit the SRR had two battalions in Bicol, one in northern Luzon, and one in Mindinao; two independent companies were in northern Luzon, two in the Visayas, one in southern Luzon, one in Mindinao, and four were being rotated through refresher training.

In August 1987 Scout Ranger students and instructors took part in an abortive coup attempt by Army Col. Gregorio Honassan. Since the previous August, however, the Scout Ranger School had once again been absorbed by the Philippines Army Training Command. Scout Rangers at the Training Command, therefore, were on detached duty from the SRR and the regiment itself was not implicated in the coup attempt. On 1 September 1987 the Scout Ranger Training Center was returned as an organic part of the SRR. Its permanent base is Fort Magsaysay, 70 miles north of Manila near Palayan City. By November 1987 the SRR consisted of four battalions, 11 independent companies, and one fire support company.

As 1988 opened Ranger elements were involved in all major engagements with the NPA. In early December Rangers were heli-lifted into Kolocot. On 6 December Rangers involved in Operation 'Red Sphinx' were inserted on the shores of Patalungan Island in Quezon to successfully intercept an NPA gun-running attempt along the coast.

The strains caused by the Communist insurgency temporarily forced Scout Ranger training to be cut from five months to three. By 1989, however, training was increased to six months. Training took place at Fort Magsaysay and was broken into five segments: individual, team, combat manoeuvre, field exercise, and test mission phase. The test mission portion usually lasted up to two months and had to involve actual contact with enemy forces in order for the class to graduate. The intensive training and retraining of the Scout Rangers had a positive effect: only 32 Rangers died during 99 encounters in 1987, a significantly better casualty rate than the Army average. In 1988 only 23 Rangers died in 166 encounters. What was notable is that almost 95 per cent of the encounters were initiated by the Rangers, proving their ability to move undetected deep into enemy territory.

Airborne and scuba training was provided for select members of the regiment. Scout Rangers regularly co-trained with foreign élite forces. In 1979, for example, the SRG held 'Lion's Den' joint exercises with the Australian Special Air Service. Rangers also train other Philippine military and paramilitary forces in Ranger tactics. The SRR's participation in an unsuccessful December 1989 coup attempt led to their effective disbandment.

MSSG member assigned to the Malaysian Army Training Centre. He wears an MSSG green beret, subdued cloth wings, and a GERAKHAS tab over the left pocket.

Army Special Forces

In the latter part of 1950 the Philippine Army organized an Airborne Battalion to be employed against Huk bands operating in Luzon. Organizational problems proved insurmountable, however, and the battalion was soon converted to regular infantry.

In early 1958 the Army designated a team to work with the US Army Special Forces to determine the feasibility of raising SF units in the event of renewed insurgency. From 1958 until 1961 the SF concept was slowly injected into the training programme of the Philippine Army; and on 21 December 1961 11 Special Forces Team was activated under the Philippine Army Training School. On 1 April of the following year the Team was brought up to strength with select personnel, most of whom were graduates of the Advanced Ranger Course (attached to the Philippine Army School Center as a Mobile Training Team).

On 25 June 1962 a second SF unit, 1 Special Forces Company (Airborne), was activated. Of the first 32 officers, 182 enlisted men, and 209 trainees, only 13 officers, 72 enlisted men, and 22 trainees qualified and were accepted into the Group. Whereas 11 SF Team was a training unit, 1 SF Group was tasked with internal defence and external employment. Training consisted of courses in Special Operations, Ranger, Airborne, Communications, Medical, Weapons, Demolition, and Intelligence. Later in the year a US Army SF Mobile Training Team conducted 20 weeks of training with 11 SF Team and 1 SF Company.

In February 1964 1 SF Co. was used on its first counter-insurgency operations in Sulu. The Group was next sent for

Malaysian PASKAL troops practise storming the beach.

civic action duty in central Luzon. Philippine Army Headquarters authorized the company to expand to an SF Group effective 1 August 1964. The Group was a Task Force-type organization, initially composed of 1 SF Company (Airborne), the Parachute Supply and Maintenance Platoon, and 'A' Company, 10 Battalion Combat Team, 1 Infantry Division. In March 1965 the Civic Action Center was also attached to the SF Group.

The SF Group was soon plagued by manpower shortages, the effect of SF members being sent to 1 Philippines Civic Action Group, Vietnam (PHILCAG). The SF Group, as a result, had to focus on training new volunteers to refill its ranks. In addition, high-altitude low-opening (HALO) free-fall parachuting and scuba training courses were initiated for select members, producing the first skydivers and combat swimmers in the Philippine Army. By June 1966 1 SF Group was again declared operational, only to lose half of its strength to the PHILCAG Replacement Unit in July 1967.

In mid-June 1968 the special forces were thrust into the limelight when it was revealed they were training anti-Malaysian rebels at a secret camp in Corregidor for infiltration into the contested Malaysian province of Sabah. President Marcos claimed the operation was not officially sanctioned and put several SF officers under arrest. The name 'Special Forces' was changed to 'Home Defense Forces' in order to save its integrity and avoid deactivation of the unit.

Home Defense Forces

As with the USSF, Home Defense Forces Group (Airborne) was divided into operational detachments, or 'A' Teams, controlled by headquarters elements, or 'B' Teams. In August 1968 a 'B' Team and five 'A' Teams were sent for disaster relief operations after the Mayon Volcano erupted. The remainder of the Group concentrated on training missions. In March 1969 1 HDF Company was operationally attached to Task

Force Habagat in Mindinao during combat against 'Black Shirt' rebels.

Student activism rocked the country in January 1970, and the entire HDFG was attached to Task Force Pasig of the Presidential Security Command. After a month the Group was pulled out, with only 2 HDF Co. left behind to perform presidential security duties. In February 1970 the remainder of the HDFG was reduced to company strength in conjunction with the reorganization plan of the Philippine Army; authorized strength was set at 25 officers and 195 enlisted personnel. Not until June 1975 was the unit reorganized once more into a Group of five operational companies plus one headquarters company. HDFG headquarters was at Fort Magsaysay.

The years 1971-75 saw the HDFG involved in heavy combat. In June 1971 one 'A' Team was attached to 10 Infantry Bn. as the striking spearhead of Task Force Barnay in the north-eastern part of the country. Two 'A' Teams were dispatched to Task Force Pagkakaisa in the south, and turned in excellent performances during battles in Mindinao. On 24 July 1974, for example, an 'A' Team defending the town of Nuro successfully withstood attacks by several hundred Muslim rebels. Meanwhile, enemy action on the shores of Palanan prompted the sealift of one 'B' Team and four 'A' Teams into the vicinity. These teams eventually became the striking force of 1/1 Bde., 1 Infantry Division, and in May 1975 were increased to form 1 HDF Company.

PASKAL on parade. They are armed with the M-16 and wear navy blue shirts and black pants with purple berets.

Special Warfare Brigade

In June 1976 the HDFG was made organic to the newly activated Philippine Army Training Command. On 16 July 1978 the HDFG, by then numbering nine companies, was absorbed into the new Army Special Warfare Brigade (SWB). Other units within the SWB were the Scout Ranger Group, Special Operations Group (SOG), and 41 and 45 Infantry Battalions. In addition, an Army Aviation Battalion was attached to the SWB in October 1978. As part of the SWB the HDFG was tasked with training and administering village defence units such as the Civilian Home Defense Forces and Special Para-Military Forces in the southern Philippines. The HDFG was also responsible for civic action programmes in the south. These efforts were responsible for bringing in 85 Muslim ralliers with 75 weapons in 1979.

The SOG, an urban warfare commando unit numbering three companies, was composed largely of HDFG veterans. Seven SOG members were sent in 1980 to Nationalist China for specialized training. Commanded by a lieutenant-colonel, the SOG conducted civil disturbance training for Scout Ranger detachments and participated in counter-insurgency operations in central Luzon.

On 1 June 1983 the SWB was disbanded and the HDFG was assigned as a separate unit under the Philippine Army

Malaysian HANDAU recruits receive their blue berets after successfully completing commando training.

Headquarters. The SOG was absorbed into the new Scout Ranger Regiment as its 6, 7, and 8 Independent Companies.

In August 1984 Armed Forces Chief of Staff Fabian Ver proposed the creation of a rapid-deployment airborne brigade drawn from the Military Police. Although Ver claimed that three battalions had been formed by the following month, the brigade, in reality, never progressed past the planning stage.

During the February 1986 Revolution most of the HDFG was in the southern Philippines administering para-military forces. The HDFG rear headquarters in Manila's Fort Bonifacio, however, declared its loyalty to the anti-Marcos rebels on 25 February.

In late 1986 the HDFG was briefly redesignated the People's Defense Regiment before reverting back to HDFG. On 1 October 1986 the Riverine Battalion (Seaborne) was absorbed by the HDFG, thereby expanding its mission and capabilities to shoreline defence.

Since late 1987 one HDFG company has been operating in each of the 12 military regions in a paramilitary training role. The Group is generally not tasked with special operations, raids, or anti-terrorist missions. Although the 'B' Team designation is no longer used, operational detachments were still called 'A' Teams. 'A' Team composition and doctrine generally follows that of the USSF. Because of the war, HDFG training has been cut from six to four months. Training, conducted at Fort Magsaysay, must include airborne quali-fication. Cross-training has been conducted with the USSF and the Australian Special Air Service. In 1989, the HDFG successfully lobbied to revert officially to the designation 'Special Forces'.

Constabulary

The Philippine Constabulary (PC) was created in the early 1950s as a supplement to the National Police. As part of the Armed Forces of the Philippines, it closely resembles the Army in its structure and function.

During the mid-1960s the PC formed an assortment of mobile Ranger units. In December 1967, for example, PC Rangers participated in anti-Communist sweeps in San Luis and Pampanga during Operation 'Denial'. These Rangers were light infantry units specializing in jungle warfare, but lacked the intensive training of the Army's Scout Rangers of the 1950s.

In 1967 the PC also formed its own Special Forces (Airborne) to improve the constabulary's special operations capabilities. Starting with a provisional company at Head-quarters level, the force developed into an SF Group of five companies: one at the national level and one each for the four PC zones prevailing at the time. Long-range plans called for one SF 'A' Team to be assigned to each province, but these plans were cancelled after the Constabulary SF got involved in partisan politics during the 1969 elections. As a result the SF Group, also known as the SF Brigade, was disbanded.

In 1972, Brig. Gen. Fidel Ramos took command of the PC. A former commander of the Army's 1 SF Co., Ramos encouraged the formation of élite units within the PC. In March 1979 one such non-airborne unit, 57 PC Ranger Bn.,

South Vietnam:
1: Brig. Gen. Doan Van Quang, LLDB, 1966
2: Private, 81 Airborne Ranger Bn., 1968
3: Lieutenant Junior Grade, LLDN SEAL, 1971

A

South Vietnam:
1: Lieutenant, SMS, 1972
2: Captain, Liaison Service, 1972
3: NCO, 81 Airborne Ranger Group, 1974

B

Indonesia:
1: Private, PGT, 1963
2: Sergeant, KOPASGAT, 1969
3: Sergeant, PASKHAS, 1984

C

Indonesia:
1: Major, KOSTRAD, 1983
2: Private, KOPASSANDHA, 1981
3: Lieutenant, BRIMOB, 1983

D

Indonesia:
1: Commando, KIPAM, 1986
2: Private, Detachment 81, 1989
3: Major, KOSTRAD, 1989

E

Thailand:
1: Sergeant, Thai Special Forces, 1989
2: Special Colonel, Thai SF, 1988
3: Captain, PARU, 1971

F

Thailand:
1: NCO, Thai Air Force CCT, 1987
2: NCO, Thai Navy SEAL, 1989
3: Lieutenant, Marine Recon, 1989

G

Malaysia:
1: NCO, MSSG, 1988
2: Lieutenant, SWTC, 1983
3: MSSG shoulder insignia

H

Malaysia:
1: NCO, HANDAU, 1988
2: Commando, PASKAL, 1988
3: HANDAU beret badge
4: PASKAL beret badge

Philippines:
1: Lieutenant, SWAG, 1984
2: NCO, HDFG, 1978
3: Staff Sergeant, SAF, 1986

J

Philippines:
1: NCO, SAF, 1987
2: Sergeant, HDFG, 1987
3: Sergeant, SRR, 1986

K

People's Republic of Vietnam:
1: Dac Cong paratrooper, 1985
2: Dac Cong Commando, 1986
3: Dac Cong insignia
4: Parachute insignia

L

was involved in heavy action against Muslim insurgents in Mindinao.

In 1983 Ramos formed his own loyal airborne PC unit, the battalion-sized Special Action Force (SAF). Included within the SAF were former members of the deactivated SF Brigade. As the national mobile strike force under the Headquarters of the PC, the SAF was tasked with conducting counter-insurgency, anti-terrorism, and the training of other PC units in specialized courses. Ramos remained close to the SAF, conducting several publicity parachute jumps with the unit during 1985. During one jump in October of that year he led 62 SAF commandos into the Bicol garrison with medical supplies. The SAF also kept at least one strike company on combat operations in the main island groups of Luzon and the Visayas.

During the 1986 Revolution the SAF played a significant role. The anti-Marcos rebels in the military, led by Ramos, were headquartered in the PC's Manila base, Camp Crame, with two companies of the SAF providing them with tactical muscle. Armed with anti-tank weapons, the SAF commandos were slated to be used as mobile strike teams if Marcos had succeeded in attacking the camp with loyal Army units.

Following the Revolution the SAF remained close to Manila, being used as the PC contingency force in the Metro Manila Capital Region. In January 1987 they played a key role in conducting the counter-siege against renegade soldiers holding the Channel 7 television compound and a hotel in Manila. During the failed August 1987 coup attempt by Army Col. Honasan the SAF launched successful ground assaults against a rebel-held hotel and radio station in the capital. And

when a top NPA commander escaped from detention in Manila's Camp Crame in November 1988, two SAF companies were temporarily assigned to guard duty around the Camp's stockade.

The SAF has also seen combat against the NPA and Muslim insurgents in recent years. In October 1987, for example, SAF elements were airlifted into Bicol during heavy fighting with the NPA; and in January 1989 13 SAF officers and 60 enlisted men were rushed to the Mindinao city of Zamboanga to retake a PC headquarters captured by renegade Muslim policemen. In March 1989 SAF detachments were rushed to Zamboanga and Dumaguete to strengthen military and police forces in these areas following reports of impending NPA attacks.

The SAF currently is commanded by a PC major and is maintained at battalion strength. As of March 1989 it had participated in over 50 campaigns in 30 of the Philippines' 68 provinces. The SAF conducts numerous training courses for its own members as well as for other PC volunteers. These include the PC Ranger Course, Basic Airborne, SCUBA, Anti-terrorism, and Special Operations Team Training.

Navy Special Forces

In 1972, the Philippine Navy created an Underwater Operations Unit (UOU) as a counterpart to the US SEALs. The unit, led by a Navy commander, was used in Mindinao against Muslim rebels in the early 1970s. One July 1973 operation on Basilan Island earned the Gold Cross Medal for

HANDAU member with M-203 grenade launcher. Note blue beret with Special Service badge on HANDAU flash. His rucksack is made from Malaysian camouflage material.

an UOU officer and 13 men after infiltrating and destroying an enemy fortification.

In 1983 the UOU was renamed the Special Warfare Group (SWAG), divided into SEAL Teams. During peacetime the SWAG was charged with seaborne rescue and salvage missions; in combat, with ship infiltration, demolitions, and unconventional amphibious operations. The SWAG is headed by a Navy commander.

In March 1988 one officer and 13 enlisted men were assigned with guarding the prison ship in Manila harbour holding renegade army Col. Honnasan. On 2 April, however, the SWAG personnel helped Honnasan escape and themselves deserted. The SWAG members were later captured.

SWAG training lasts six months and, according to official Philippine publications, has a 75 to 90 per cent dropout rate. Training includes courses in demolitions, cartography, scuba, parachuting, and hand-to-hand combat. As with the US SEALs, trainees must undergo a 'Hell Week' before entrance

into the unit. The SWAG regularly co-trains with the US SEALs, and together they conduct annual amphibious exercises codenamed PALAU.

In addition to the SWAG, the Philippine Marines have airborne-qualified detachments, including an airborne Quick Reaction Force during the early 1980s.

Singapore

In 1967 Maj. Tan Kim Peng was sent to the US for airborne and ranger training. Upon his return a Commando Unit was activated under his command. By 1971, the airborne-qualified unit was expanded into 1 Commando Battalion.

Because of Singapore's small size, limiting training facilities, 1 Cdo. Bn. has been forced to go overseas for much of its training. In February 1972 the battalion commander and a second officer went to the US for seven months of training; after completing Jumpmaster, Freefall, and Freefall Jumpmaster courses, the commander returned to Singapore, the second officer remaining to act as liaison for a second group of officers arriving in late 1972. At the same time other members of the battalion received training from the UK, Israel, and Australia.

In August 1973, six officers and 22 NCOs arrived at Lopburi for a six-week jungle warfare course with the Royal Thai Special Forces. They were trained in long-range reconnaissance techniques during field exercises at Kanchanaburi, Sattahip, and Chieng Mai. On 3 November 1973 142 members of the battalion went to New Zealand for co-training with the New Zealand Special Air Service at Whangaparoa Camp in Auckland. The students included a platoon of regulars, the remainder being national servicemen. The ten weeks of training covered basic commando techniques, section and platoon training, and joint exercises with the NZSAS acting as aggressors. In July 1974 the Singaporean Armed Forces opened a Parachute School at Changi Airport and began qualifying all members of the battalion. The four-week course included an advanced class in HALO techniques. Nine jumps were required for wings to be awarded.

In mid-April 1989 almost 300 members of the battalion participated in Neptune 89 joint exercises with 1 New Zealand Infantry Regiment in north-eastern Singapore. Commando trainees are also regularly sent to Thailand for airborne training.

A second reservist battalion was raised in the mid-seventies as part of Singapore's 200,000-strong national reserves.

Singapore's commandos are disciplined but untested. In 1974 and again in 1987 the battalion was presented with the annual Best Combat Unit award. However, they have yet to see combat against either external or internal enemies. In the event of war the commandos, like the rest of the armed forces, will be used defensively to inflict a prohibitively high cost on a foreign invader.

Commando personnel are identified by red berets with metal national insignia pinned on the left side. Singaporean wings are worn over the left breast; foreign wings go over the right breast. A shoulder insignia bearing a winged dagger was worn until the early 1980s; currently, armed forces regulations authorize no shoulder insignia. US-style leaf pattern camouflage is worn as standard combat dress.

Thailand: Police Special Forces

Concerned about the threat to Thai security after the fall of China in 1949, the US helped the Thai Police establish an élite airborne cadre in 1950. Tasked with conducting operations in remote areas, the 50-man cadre had extensive language skills to help it operate among minority hilltribes. In June 1951 the cadre became involved in Thai domestic politics when Royal Thai Navy rebels kidnapped the Prime Minister aboard its flagship, the destroyer *Sri Ayuthaya*. The rebels positioned the flagship across from Bangkok and began shelling Police and Army buildings. The élite Police cadre was then put into action; a mortar round scored a direct hit, setting the *Sri Ayuthaya* on fire. The Prime Minister leapt from the ship and swam ashore, ending the apparent coup attempt.

That July the powerful Chief of Police, Gen. Phao, seized control of Bangkok in a coup d'état. With Phao's consent the US began expanding the Police airborne cadre into a paramilitary élite outside the normal Police chain of command. The new formation, called the Police Aerial Resupply Unit (PARU), specialized in covert operations in isolated areas, including long-range reconnaissance, intelligence-collecting, and sabotage missions. PARU was commanded by a Police colonel and listed—on paper—as subordinate to the Border Patrol Police. PARU established an airborne training camp at Lopburi, 93 miles north of Bangkok. There it began

recruiting volunteers from the Army, Navy and Police. Three US civilian advisors were formally given officer ranks within the unit. By the end of 1953 over 300 PARU commandos had been trained. During the same year recruiting was restricted to the Navy and Police, signalling a growing rivalry between the Police and Army.

PARU forged close links with the Thai royal family. In 1953 it moved its training camp and headquarters to Camp Narusuan at Hua Hin, next to one of the royal palaces. In part because of its association with the king, PARU was able to send a handful of students annually to the Royal Thai Army Officer Candidate School, a privilege previously only extended to élite families. PARU saw action as early as 1952 against opium warlords in the north-east. In 1954 it also provided training for small numbers of palace guards for the newly independent Republic of Vietnam.

In September 1957 PARU suffered a setback when Police Gen. Phao was overthrown in an Army-led coup. Phao's enormous empire was divided, and PARU were threatened with disbandment. Because of its royal links, however, PARU avoided dissolution.

PARU operations in Laos

The unit's fortunes improved in 1960 with the growing crisis in neighboring Laos. Thailand grew understandably concerned with the situation across its border and in December sent two PARU teams to assist during the Royal Lao government's

Malaysian VAT 69 members in training. They wear standard Police Field Force olive drab fatigue.

47

Thai Marine Recon HAHO (High Altitude-High Opening) and HALO parachutists.

conducting reconnaissance and raids along the northern Ho Chi Minh Trail.

Because of heavy casualties suffered in combat since 1961, PARU was seriously weakened by the late 1960s. After a retraining programme, PARU was rebuilt by mid-1969 into a 700-man battalion composed of ten detachments. In addition, the unit had an air and sea rescue section; the former was inserted into Laos to recover bodies from an aircraft crash in 1967.

In the early 1970s, Thailand became concerned with Cambodia's Khmer Rouge insurgency, and PARU teams were sent on cross-border reconnaissance operations into enemy-held sections of the Khmer Republic.

Following 1975, Thailand's attention turned to the threat from its own Communist insurgency. In late 1976 PARU joined with the Border Patrol Police on operations against left-wing guerrillas along its southern border with Malaysia.

Since the late 1970s PARU's missions have been limited. As new members were inducted into the force, many of its experienced Lao veterans have been removed. This heightened tensions between young and old PARU members, prompting a December 1986 revolt at Camp Narusuan. As a result of this incident PARU veterans have been retained in the unit. Since then, PARU has seen limited action against separatist bandits in southern Thailand during June 1988.

Border Patrol Police

In addition to PARU, Border Patrol Police (BPP) units contain substantial numbers of airborne and ranger-qualified personnel. As early as September 1960 US Army SF in Okinawa trained ten BPP students in ranger tactics. Two US SF Mobile Training Teams arrived in Okinawa during March and April 1961 to train 60 more BPP members. By 1964 the BPP was being retrained and expanded for counter-

Plaque outside company headquarters of the Thai Marine Recon Battalion's Amphibious Reconnaissance Company.

successful recapture of Vientiane. In January 1961 PARU was assigned to assist pro-government Laotian guerrillas in north-eastern Laos. Three groups of five PARU commandos were chosen from its Pathfinder platoon and inserted around the Plain of Jars to begin training the irregular forces of the Hmong hilltribe commander, Lt.Col. Vang Pao. By mid-1961 99 PARU operatives were in northern Laos. Total PARU strength stood at 550 men. At Camp Narusuan PARU was training Hmong Special Operations Teams; by 1962 the first battalion-sized Hmong Special Guerrilla Unit had been trained. In the same year a 30-man cadre from the Laotian paramilitary Directorate of National Co-ordination (DNC) went to Narusuan for airborne training.

In 1963 PARU began to come under pressure from Thailand's Army-controlled government. Because of an agreement made immediately after the 1957 coup, PARU was charged with building a training camp in the northern town of Phitsanulok. PARU was to contribute personnel to a joint Police–Army Special Battalion to be stationed at the camp, with plans for the eventual full integration of PARU into the battalion. Command of the Special Battalion went to an Army Special Forces officer, with one deputy from PARU and one from Special Forces. In 1964 the battalion began offering commando and guerrilla training to foreign students. Laotian and Cambodian units passed through its courses before training ceased in 1975.

Although some PARU personnel were transferred to the Special Battalion, PARU resisted integration and kept the bulk of its force at Hua Hin. By the mid-1960s, PARU had expanded its Laotian training mission both in northern Laos and at Hua Hin. In addition, select detachments were insurgency (CI) operations. US Army SF provided 12-month CI courses for 500 picked BPP members in 1964. The BPP numbered over 3,000 by that time, many of them airborne trained. The BPP expanded to over 8,000 men by mid-1969, with virtually all of its members trained as a CI force. BPP elements, together with PARU, operated in north-western Thailand in the late 1960s against Communist terrorists and opium warlords. The BPP also provided instructors for the training of Laotian irregulars inside Laos and in Thailand.

BPP operations against CTs and Malaysian-based Communists continued into the 1970s. In the 1980s, heliborne BPP units fought against the opium warlord Khun Sa's Shan United Army in the Golden Triangle region.

Army Special Forces

In 1953 the first US Army advisors arrived in Thailand to help the Royal Thai Army set up an airborne formation. In that year Camp Erawan was established at Lopburi for the fledgling parachute unit. The site had been previously occupied by the PARU, which had since moved down to Hua Hin. In the same year Capt. Tienchai Sirisumpan, a company commander in the King's Guard Regiment, was sent as one of the first foreign students to US Army Ranger training at Fort Benning, Georgia. Tienchai returned to Thailand the following year and was given command in 1955 of the newly designated Airborne Ranger Unit. In 1956 the Rangers were used together with the BPP on operations along the southern border with British Malaya. During the following year, the Unit secured the capital as Police Gen. Phao was overthrown by Army commander Field Marshal Sarit.

By that time, the Rangers had expanded into an Airborne Ranger Battalion numbering 580 men divided into 26 detachments. Over the next few years the paratroopers conducted field operations throughout the northern provinces, identifying loyal village leaders in the event of a Communist insurgency similar to the ones growing elsewhere in South-East Asia.

The deteriorating situation in Laos soon commanded the attention of the Rangers. In July 1959 interpreters from the Rangers were sent to Vientiane to begin assisting the Laotian army. These forces were temporarily assigned to Headquarters 333, Thailand's command unit for missions in Laos. Meanwhile, the Laotian 2e Bataillon Parachutiste was sent in November to Lopburi for refresher training. The Laotian 1er Bataillon Parachutiste arrived at Lopburi in mid-1960, but was rushed back after the 2 BP rebelled and took over the capital. In 1961 radio operators and other specialists were sent from the Ranger Battalion to assist the Lao army.

In 1963 the Airborne Ranger Battalion was expanded and renamed the Special Forces Group (Airborne). Composed of six companies, the new Group was tasked with unconventional warfare behind enemy lines, psychological warfare operations, counter-insurgency missions, and the raising of village defence units.

The Royal Thai Special Forces (RTSF) resumed the training of Lao military units in 1965 when parachute and infantry battalions arrived for refresher training at Camp Erawan, Lopburi. In the same year the first two RTSF

Thai Marine Recon static line parachutists wearing leaf camouflage fatigues.

training teams were sent to northern Laos to train local forces. One Thai sergeant was captured from these teams in May, and was not to be released until 1974. RTSF recon teams also started operating along the Ho Chi Minh Trail.

1966 to 1975

In 1966, US Army SF units arrived in Lopburi and began working extensively with the RTSF. By that time an RTSF Special Warfare Center had been established at Camp Narai, Lopburi, with 1 and 2 SF Groups (Airborne). The Special Warfare Commander was Col. Tienchai; SF Groups were commanded by colonels. In addition, 1 Airborne Battalion, commanded by a lieutenant-colonel, and the Quartermaster Aerial Resupply Company came under SWC command at Camp Erawan. The Airborne Battalion's mission was to provide airborne infantry reinforcements for the Army's conventional units.

The RTSF's Laotian missions continued through the late 1960s, with liaison and mobile training teams assigned across Laos. One team was with the Nam Bac garrison when it fell in January 1968; all personnel were rescued after evading enemy patrols for a week. The RTSF also assigned men to 1 Long Range Reconnaissance Troop of the Royal Thai Army Expeditionary Division, Vietnam, from 1969-1971.

By 1971 the widening war in South-East Asia provided the RTSF with more training missions. The RTSF already ran the Special Warfare School at Lopburi, which included airborne training facilities and a ranger course modelled after the US Army Ranger School. By this time the RTSF training facilities were considered among the best in Asia.

The RTSF stayed involved in Laos, training Lao personnel

Thai Marine Recon team prepares to jump with wardogs.

at Lopburi until 1973 and occasionally sending teams on reconnaissance operations inside Laos. Other RTSF personnel manned the Special Battalion at Phitsanulok, which trained foreign students and conducted cross-border operations. The RTSF also provided men for the Palace Guard in Bangkok. In addition, RTSF Mobile Training Teams spanned Thailand, conducting civic-action projects and training local anti-Communist militia.

In 1972 the SWC had expanded further with the creation of 3 SF Group (Airborne). Also in the SWC were 1 and 2 SF Groups, the Special Warfare School, 1 Airborne Battalion, the Quartermaster Aerial Resupply Company, the Psychological Operations Battalion, and the Long Range Reconnaissance Company. The Special Warfare Commander was Maj. Gen. Tienchai.

In the final years of the Vietnam War, Thailand was confronted with hostile Communist movements in both Laos and the Khmer Republic. RTSF teams were used on recon operations in Khmer Rouge-held territory along the northern half of the Khmer border. No RTSF personnel were lost on these missions.

RTSF post-Vietnam

By 1977 4 SF Group (Airborne) had been raised to strength at Phitsanulok after the Special Battalion was fully absorbed by the RTSF. In the same year 1 Airborne Battalion was taken from the SWC and put under the command of 31 Regiment, 1st Division (King's Guard). In the late 1970s the RTSF was involved with training local village militia units during the

height of the Communist Party of Thailand (CPT) insurgency. RTSF teams also conducted cross-border operation into Cambodia to gain intelligence on CPT training camps se up by the sympathetic Khmer Rouge regime.

The RTSF stayed active as a training unit in the early 1980s. Besides helping raise Thai paramilitary militia, the RTSF also provided assistance to the anti-Communist Cambodian resistance as early as 1979, with expanded programmes for the Khmer People's National Liberation Fron and the National Sihanoukist Army since 1982. Among othe recent missions of the RTSF have been operations along the Cambodian border (prior to October 1987 co-ordinated through Army Operations Center 315), missions along the Laotian border (previously under AOC 309), and strike against Burmese opium warlords. In the mid-1980s the RTSF trained members of Task Force 838, an élite unit that oversee the activities of the Cambodian resistance along the Thai Cambodian border.

In July 1982 the four Special Forces Groups under the SWC were renamed 1, 2, 3, and 4 Special Forces Regiments of Special Forces Division (Airborne). At the same time the entire 31 Regt. of the 1st Division, which controlled Airborne Battalion co-located at Camp Erawan, was redesig nated 31 Airborne Regt. 1st Division. The regiment i currently headquartered at Lopburi, with one airborn battalion rotated through Camp Erawan.

In 1984 the Special Warfare Command was established a Lopburi to co-ordinate all Thai Army élite units. With external threats to Thailand's security from Cambodia, Laos Vietnam and Burma, the Command is given responsibility for waging war outside the borders of the country. The Specia

Warfare Command is also known as 5 Army Region, marking it as a lieutenant-general's command equal to the four geographical Army Regions.

While not prone to involvement in Thai domestic politics, the RTSF dispatched 11 helicopter-loads of paratroopers to Bangkok during a September 1985 coup attempt. Their intervention was largely symbolic, however, since the government was already well in control by the time they arrived. In May 1986 the RTSF was again poised for intervention in Bangkok when Army commander-in-chief Arthit appeared ready to launch a coup.

Although minor counter-terrorist missions were assumed by units of the paramilitary Rangers (not to be confused with ranger graduates of the RTSF Special Warfare School) in August 1984, the RTSF is responsible for responding to major terrorist incidents and hostage-rescue situations. In 1989 RTSF counter-terrorist missions were handled by Task Force 90, based in Lopburi.

The RTSF maintains links with SF units around the world. Several joint training exercises are conducted annually with the US Army Special Forces. Exchange training programmes are held with the Australian SAS and the South Korean SF, among others. In addition to training their own personnel, the RTSF provides instructors for Royal Thai Army Ranger courses located at the SWC, the Infantry Training Center, and the Cavalry Training Center. All RTSF members must be graduates of the nine-week course.

With over three decades of combat experience, the RTSF today stands as one of the most capable élite forces in Asia. In 1989 the RTSF fielded two full divisions. The Special Warfare

Command and the SWC remain at Lopburi. 1 SF Division is headquartered at Camp Erawan, with one of its regiments at each of Lopburi's three military camps: 1 SF Regt. at Camp Pawai, 2 SF Regt. at Camp Narai, and 3 SF Regt. at Camp Erawan. 2 SF Division moved its permanent headquarters to Chieng Mai in early 1988, having been temporarily quartered at Lopburi over the previous year. The division has two regiments: 4 SF Regt., formerly the Special Battalion, at Phitsanulok, and 5 SF Regt. at Chieng Mai. The Long Range Reconnaissance Company, Airborne Resupply Battalion and Psychological Operations Battalion, which seconded personnel in 1988 to the Displaced Persons Protection Unit along the Thai-Cambodian border, are also at Camp Erawan.

Marine Recon

In 1965 the Royal Thai Marine Corps formed a reconnaissance company with the mission of conducting ground and amphibious reconnaissance and special operations. On 27 November 1978, the company was expanded into the Recon Battalion. The battalion currently consists of one headquarters company with an attached platoon of wardogs, one amphibious reconnaissance company, and two V-150 patrol vehicle companies. The unit is headed by an RTMC lieutenant-colonel and is based at Sattahip.

A handful of Marine Recon members saw combat when sent to Laos as part of volunteer Bn. Cdo. 619 which fought on the Plain of Jars in 1972. As a unit, companies from the battalion are assigned to the RTMC regiments as needed.

Thai Marine Recon anti-terrorist team, 1988.

One company was attached in 1989 to an RTMC Task Force at Chanthaburi for operations along the Thai-Cambodian border.

Recon personnel are airborne-qualified at the RTMC parachute school at Sattahip; eight jumps are made, including one night and two water jumps. Recon personnel must also attend the three-month amphibious reconnaissance course at Sattahip covering land and sea tactics.

Navy SEAL

The Royal Thai Navy SEALs trace their origin back to the first Thai combat diver unit created in 1956. In 1965 the unit was expanded and re-organized with US Navy assistance. Three years later the unit was again re-organized with US Navy assistance, splitting personnel between an Underwater Demolitions Team and a SEAL (Sea, Air, Land) Team. UDTs are assigned salvage operations, obstacle clearance, and underwater demolitions; the SEALs, reconnaissance and intelligence missions.

Thai SEALs undergo six months of intensive training at Sattahip. All members are airborne-qualified; parachute training is conducted at the RTMC Airborne School or Army Airborne course at Lopburi. Additional special warfare courses are provided by the RTSF at Lopburi. The SEALs are headed by a navy commander and consist of 144 officers and men divided into SEAL Teams 1 and 2. Each Team is further sub-divided into four smaller reconnaissance teams.

Thai SEALs have been used to gather intelligence during periods of heightened tension along Thailand's borders. In December 1978, for example, recon teams were sent to the Mekong River during skirmishes with the Pathet Lao. The SEALs also participate in anti-piracy operations in the Gulf of Thailand.

Air Force Special Forces

The Royal Thai Air Force has a combined SF unit within 201

Thai Marine Recon Battalion shoulder insignia.

Sqn. (Helicopter), 2 Wing, at Lopburi. The unit, numbering less than 100 men, is responsible for para-rescue, combat control missions, and anti-terrorist operations around airports. In early 1988 a heliborne detachment rescued a Thai fighter pilot shot down along the border during hostilities with Laos. During April–May 1988, 43 members from the unit held 'Badge Tram 88' field exercises in Thailand with a US Air Force Combat Team.

Socialist Republic of Vietnam

As part of its expansion efforts in the late 1950s, the People's Army of Vietnam (PAVN) sent students to both the USSR and China for airborne training. These cadres returned to Vietnam in 1958 to form the nucleus of a parachute unit. The unit was not used in any combat activity either inside North Vietnam or in neighbouring countries.

In 1962 the unit was expanded into *Lu Doan Nhay Du 305* (305 Airborne Brigade) with a strength of 1,400 officers and men; minus headquarters and support personnel, this number allowed for only two understrength battalions. However, by setting the unit at brigade strength, the paratroopers were theoretically authorized a larger TO&E and higher-ranking officer cadre than a standard PAVN infantry regiment; following normal PAVN practice, command of the brigade was probably held by a lieutenant-colonel. The brigade was based near Hanoi and conducted airborne training exercises from air force An-2, Li-2, and Il-14 transports. Weapons as large as 12.7mm anti-aircraft artillery and 82mm mortars were also dropped during training. Many jumps were held at night to avoid interception by US fighter aircraft.

In 1964 the brigade began to lose strength as paratroopers were transferred to non-airborne sapper units. In 1966 a prisoner captured near Nha Trang, who had himself received airborne training in the USSR and was a former officer in the brigade, revealed that most of 305 Abn. Bde. had been dispersed to sapper formations during the previous year. The brigade continued on paper until finally dissolved in 1968; it had never been used in combat.

The 305 *Dac Cong* ('Special Task') Command, also known as 305 Sapper Command, was officially created in 1967 as an administrative umbrella for PAVN special operations units. The *Dac Cong* traced their lineage from the Viet Minh demolition soldiers of the First Indochina War. By the mid-1960s, however, the *Dac Cong* more closely resembled assault or shock troops akin to the British Commandos and US Army Rangers of World War Two.

In practice, 305 Sapper Command directly controlled the Sapper Training School at Xuan Mai 50 miles south-west of Hanoi, and a small number of reserve special operations detachments. The Xuan Mai facilities had previously been the headquarters of 338 Division, the initial PAVN infiltration division into South Vietnam.

The vast majority of *Dac Cong* formations fell under the operational control of PAVN field units. After the PAVN shifted in 1965 from a heavy infantry division TO&E to a light division concept, sapper elements were attached to each

division, regiment, battalion, and company. The sappers were soon treated in North Vietnamese publications as the élite of the PAVN. Being privileged units, they were entitled to better pay and rations. Sapper training lasted up to one year.

Dac Cong in Tet

During the 1968 Tet Offensive, PAVN and VC *Dac Cong* units saw extensive action while spearheading attacks on targets within major population centres, including attacks by the VC C-10 Sapper Battalion against the US Embassy in Saigon. Despite such highly publicized sapper attacks, the Communist forces, especially the Viet Cong, were decimated. Following Tet the *Dac Cong* underwent extensive expansion as the PAVN assumed greater direct involvement in the war in South Vietnam. Although some *Dac Cong* units specialized in urban warfare and underwater demolitions, the bulk of them were used as reconnaissance, demolitions, minefield-breaching, and shock detachments.

By late January 1973 the PAVN had over 12,000 *Dac Cong* assigned to the war in South Vietnam. Most were grouped into understrength battalions and, occasionally, regiments. Battalions numbered only 150–200 men; regiments averaged about 600 men. Viet Cong Sapper Battalions, composed in part of PAVN regulars, numbered only 100 men. In addition, 126 Naval Sapper Group of 500 men and the DMZ Sapper Group of 1,500 men were located in South Vietnam's I Corps.

Dac Cong battalions and groups were usually assigned to a military front or military region in South Vietnam. *Dac Cong* regiments were either attached to a PAVN infantry division, a military front, or a military region. In addition, 429 Sapper Command Headquarters—the *Dac Cong* reserve for attacks on the region around Saigon—controlled 29 Sapper Regt. and seven other sapper battalions.

In 1974 *Dac Cong* units remained active in South Vietnam,

Thai Air Force Combat Control Team unpacks a motorcycle after parachuting into an 'enemy-held' airfield during BADGE TRAM 87 Exercises.

including the 21 October attack by naval sappers on the Hoa An Bridge linking Bien Hoa and Saigon. The sappers floated two rafts loaded with explosives down the Dong Nai River; a rope between the rafts wrapped around a bridge pillar and knocked down two spans. During the 1975 spring offensive on Saigon, the *Dac Cong* were in the forefront of every PAVN attack. 27 Sapper Division was targeted on Tan Son Nhut Airbase in mid-April.

Operations in Laos and Cambodia

During the Second Indochina War *Dac Cong* units were also active in Laos and Cambodia. Lao operations, known in PAVN vernacular as Internationalist Mission C, were some of the most spectacular *Dac Cong* operations of the war. In March 1968, for example, a detachment from 305 *Dac Cong* Command spearheaded an assault on a US-manned radar station on Phou Pha Thi mountain in north-eastern Laos. Scaling the 5,000-foot sheer cliffs of Phou Pha Thi on ropes, the *Dac Cong* took the radar base by surprise and killed a dozen Americans. Other operations in Laos include an August 1967 raid on the southern town of Saravane; a 1969 rocket attack against the Muong Soui garrison, killing one American; and a February 1970 assault against the main Lao government outpost on the Plain of Jars. PAVN *Dac Cong* also trained counterparts in the Pathet Lao.

In Cambodia, 100 Vietnamese sappers were responsible for a spectacular January 1971 attack on Phnom Penh's Pochentong Airbase, destroying virtually the entire Cambodian Air Force. *Dac Cong* also launched the abortive October 1972 raid on an armoured vehicle park in the northern outskirts of

Thai Air Force Combat Control Team member with a Blowpipe missile during BADGE TRAM 87 Exercises.

Phnom Penh. 367 Sapper Group, also known as 367 Sapper Regt., continued operations against the Cambodian government in 1973, including an April rocket attack on Phnom Penh itself. The regiment left its base north of Phnom Penh and Cambodia in late 1973. While attached to the PAVN 5 Division the regiment spearheaded the offensive on Tay Ninh in March 1975. PAVN *Dac Cong* trained Khmer Communist sappers until 1974.

During the height of the Second Indochina War *Dac Cong* missions even extended into Thailand, including January 1972 deep-penetration attacks on Utapao and Udorn Airbases by teams from 305 *Dac Cong* Command. Following the fall of Saigon in 1975 a large influx of Soviet equipment and advisors changed the PAVN into an increasingly conventional, modern armed force. As part of this change the massive *Dac Cong* corps that had existed at the end of the Second Indochina War started to be streamlined into a smaller special operations force.

During the December 1978 PAVN blitzkrieg across Cambodia *Dac Cong* units were again in action. In the early morning of 2 January 1979 two teams crossed the Tonle Sap River by rubber boat in an attempt to kidnap Cambodian

Prince Norodom Sihanouk. The sappers were spotted and all but one were killed.

Shortly after the invasion of Cambodia the PAVN reorganized the *Dac Cong* Command at Xuan Mai into three brigades, believed to be numbered 113, 117, and 198. Each brigade contains airborne, seaborne, and long-range reconnaissance detachments. 117 Brigade is known to have rotated through Cambodia during the mid-1980s, and was probably involved in attacks against Cambodian resistance bases in March 1985. *Dac Cong* forays against Thai-based resistance camps have also been alleged.

In addition to the three *Dac Cong* brigades, specialized *Trinh Sat* ('Reconnaissance') detachments are assigned to PAVN infantry divisions and military regions. These detachments have seen action in Cambodia; for example, a recon team from PAVN 302 Division, 479 Front in Battambang Province was pictured in an August 1986 PAVN publication. PAVN often uses the terms *Dac Cong* and *Trinh Sat* interchangeably in its publications.

Such publications have also on occasion featured photos of amphibious commandos with scuba gear and rubber infiltration boats. These forces have been variously identified as belonging to 'Group X' and 'Group 10', and it is unknown if they are assigned outside the *Dac Cong* formations previously described.

Burma

In 1953, a Burmese military mission was sent to Israel to study the feasibility of training airborne instructors; six officers and three other ranks departed for training the following year. At the same time a similar agreement was reached with the US. Israeli and US advisory groups visited Burma over the next few years to help construct an airborne school. At the end of 1956 the school was established at Hmawbi, 26 miles northwest of Rangoon. Two years later a group of US instructors arrived to help run the first parachute course at Hmawbi, which began in May of that year with an initial intake of 150 trainees.

In 1958 the airborne school included two airborne assault companies. An Airborne Battalion was also established in that year at Hmawbi. By 1961 the airborne school was able to assume full responsibility for parachute training, and foreign assistance ceased.

The Airborne Battalion was used on several operations in the north against the Burmese Communist Party during the late 1960s and early 1970s. Currently it is a national reserve unit. Airborne qualification originally included five day jumps and one night jump. This was later increased to 16 jumps, though it has recently been reduced to six jumps.

The Plates

South Vietnam:
A1: Brig.Gen. Doan Van Quang, LLDB, 1966
In August 1964 Brig.Gen. Doan Van Quang was given command of the LLDB, a position he held for the next five years. He wears the green LLDB beret, with the distinctive LLDB badge adopted in 1964—this was similar to the ARVN

Airborne badge except that the wingtips curved inward instead of out. Cloth LLDB wings are worn over the right pocket; though none are worn on this uniform, honorary US jumpwings were awarded to all members of the LLDB and worn over the left pocket. The standard LLDB insignia is worn on the left shoulder. Besides the olive drab fatigues seen in the plate, photographs exist of Brig.Gen. Quang wearing an ARVN Airborne leaf camouflage uniform with matching patrol cap. Like the US Army SF LLDB members wore a mix of uniforms including olive drab fatigues, leaf pattern and tiger-stripe camouflage.

A2: Private, 81 Airborne Ranger Bn., 1968
As Project DELTA's fast reaction force, 91 Airborne Ranger Battalion was lightly equipped for mobile strike missions. When the designation was changed to 81 Airborne Ranger Battalion the unit remained outfitted as a light infantry force. Based on a 16 June 1968 photo, this commando prepares for a sweep of the suburbs north-west of Saigon. He wears Bata boots, a US M1 steel helmet, M1952 armour vest, and M1956 pistol belt with M26 grenades. LLDB insignia is worn on the left shoulder; though not visible, LLDB wings went over the right pocket.

A3: Lieutenant Junior Grade, LLDN SEAL, 1971
The uniform and equipment of the LLDN SEALs strongly reflected the influence of the US Navy SEALs. This Vietnamese wears tightly-tailored tiger-stripe fatigues and US jungle boots. The black beret and bullion beret badge were worn by the entire LLDN. Colour variations of the patch on the right pocket distinguished subordinate units within the LLDN: a red patch was worn by SEALs, green by Boat Support personnel, orange by the EOD Team, and light blue by UDT members. In 1971 the red SEAL version added the words *Hai Kich* to the upper right. LLDN SEAL wings, based on US Navy jumpwings, are worn over the right pocket. A subdued US Navy SEAL qualification badge over the left pocket indicates SEAL training in the continental United States.

Members of the Coastal Security Service, South Vietnam's other amphibious special operations unit, used 'sterile' uniforms and equipment while on missions to North Vietnam. Between missions, Vietnamese Navy elements within the CSS wore a red embroidered Vietnamese Navy cap badge (regular Vietnamese Navy personnel wore a yellow cap badge).

South Vietnam:
B1: Lieutenant, SMS, 1972
When the SMS was formed from elements of the LLDB the green LLDB beret was replaced by the red STD beret with the standard ARVN Airborne badge. (Groups 11 and 68, which were later absorbed into the SMS, briefly wore black berets in the late 1960s but soon changed to red.) Subdued rank insignia are worn on the collar of the ARVN Airborne leaf camouflage uniform. ARVN Airborne wings are worn over the right pocket; US jumpwings, awarded while a member of the LLDB, over the left pocket. On the left shoulder is the official SMS 'dragon' insignia.

B2: Captain, Liaison Service, 1972
In the field the Liaison Service employed the same mix of friendly and enemy items used by MACV-SOG. Between combat missions Service members initially wore JGS insignia on the left shoulder and the Liaison Service patch on the right

Philippines SAF practise rappelling, 1987.

pocket. After the Service was absorbed into the STD in 1968, only members of the STD headquarters were permitted to wear the JGS insignia on the left shoulder. As a result, the Liaison Service shifted their distinctive insignia to the left shoulder. (Other subordinate units of the STD, i.e., the SMS and Long Thanh Training Center, also wore their distinctive insignia on the left shoulder.) ARVN Airborne wings are worn over the right pocket; a LRRP qualification badge, awarded to graduates of a course at Long Thanh, over the left pocket. (A badge of the same design was awarded to other ARVN LRRP units for courses at other training centers.) The camouflage is a lightweight ARVN copy of the British World War Two 'Windproof' pattern, used by some French paratroop units in Indochina and later passed on to the ARVN Airborne. (The Liaison Service did not use a 'standard' uniform, part of a conscious attempt by the STD to disguise its numbers.)

B3: NCO, 81 Airborne Ranger Group, 1974
After the dissolution of the LLDB the 81 Airborne Ranger

Group was the only ex-LLDB component to retain the green beret and LLDB beret badge. The LLDB shoulder insignia was replaced by a new 81 Airborne Ranger Group patch. (Several unofficial tabs were often worn above this patch to denote specialized companies within the Group.) Because airborne training for the Group shifted from Nha Trang to Tan Son Nhut, LLDB wings were replaced by standard ARVN Airborne wings.

The Group was used as fast reaction shock force during the final years of the war and was outfitted like standard ARVN Airborne and Ranger battalions. This commando, pictured immediately prior to a heliborne insertion in December 1974, wears ARVN Airborne leaf camouflage with a cotton magazine bandolier and M1956 pistol belt.

Indonesia:
C1. Private, PGT, 1963
Prior to 1986 the Indonesians had a tradition of developing distinctive camouflage patterns for each of their élite forces. Nowhere is this more evident than with the Air Force Special Forces. The PGT wore indonesia's first camouflage uniform in a spot pattern first developed by the US forces during the World War Two Pacific campaign, then adopted by the Dutch during Indonesia's fight for independence, and finally used by Indonesia's élite units. The pistol belt is of US design. Rank insignia are worn on shoulder loops. Metal Air Force jumpwings are worn over the left pocket, an Air Force Special Forces insignia on the left shoulder. The weapon is the Belgian G-3, standard issue to the Indonesian Armed Forces during the early 1960s. As was the authorized practice at the time, the unit designation is worn over the right breast.

C2: Sergeant, KOPASGAT, 1969
After the expansion of the PGT into KOPASGAT, the Air Force paras changed their spot camouflage to a unique pattern reminiscent of Belgian camouflage. KOPASGAT also

Philippines Scout Ranger insignia: beret badge (left, top); chest qualification badge (left, bottom); unit shoulder insignia (right).

began using an orange beret with a distinctive badge. Above the cloth Air Force jumpwings is an embroidered Air Force SF qualification badge, similar to the Army Commando qualification insignia except that the wings are bigger and the word 'Commando' is on the bottom instead of the top. The Air Force SF unit insignia, identical to that of the PGT, is on the left shoulder; rank insignia are worn on shoulder loops. The weapon is the Soviet AK-47. A commando dagger is worn on the Indonesian pistol belt. The unit designation is printed on a tab over the right breast.

C3: Sergeant, PASKHAS, 1984
After KOPASGAT underwent re-organization into PASKHAS a new camouflage pattern was briefly adopted by the group before the entire armed forces switched to British Disruptive Pattern Material (DPM) in 1986. The orange beret was retained, but with a new Air Force SF badge. Subdued rank insignia are worn on the upper sleeve, and a name tag above the right pocket, replacing the unit designation. Air Force jumpwings and an Air Force SF qualification badge, both subdued, are worn over the left pocket, and a subdued Air Force SF group insignia on the left shoulder. The weapon is the M-16; an Indonesian bayonet is worn on an Indonesian pistol belt. Currently, both the M-16 and folding-stock FNC are used by PASKHAS.

Indonesia:
D1: Major, KOSTRAD, 1983
KOSTRAD paratroopers and para-raiders wore the spotted Indonesian camouflage pattern during the mid-1960s (see C1); by the late 1960s a US 'maple leaf' camouflage, developed by US forces during World War Two, was issued. Two further patterns were in use by the early 1980s: a dark vertical stripe seen on the helmet cover, and a 'brush-stroke' camouflage similar to the British Denison pattern seen on this figure's jacket. By 1984 the KOSTRAD were the first in Indonesia to begin wearing British DPM camouflage, two years before the rest of the Armed Forces standardized on this pattern. On the left shoulder is the KOSTRAD insignia with a 'KOSTRAD' tab; Indonesian airborne wings are worn over the left breast, a name tag over the right pocket, and embroidered rank on the collar.

D2: Private, KOPASSANDHA, 1981
The uniform and insignia of the Indonesian Army SF changed little between 1958 and 1986. This KOPASSANDHA commando wears the red beret and beret badge originally adopted by the RPKAD in 1958. The camouflage, first used by the RPKAD in 1964, is known as the 'Special Forces Pattern'. The sleeves have been cut and sewn to appear rolled up, a common practice in the Indonesian SF. Army airborne wings and the Army SF qualification badge over the left pocket and Para-Komando unit insignia on the left shoulder were retained since the days of the RPKAD. A Para-Komando tab is occasionally worn on the left shoulder. A name tag is worn over the right pocket. During the 1981 Woyla rescue operation the KOPASSANDHA commandos wore their red berets and SF camouflage with British body armour. Although the standard KOPASSANDHA weapon from 1977 to 1981 was the M-16, the Woyla rescue force was issued the H&K MP5.

D3: Lieutenant, BRIMOB, 1983

Although an élite formation, BRIMOB wears its black beret slanted to the left, an Indonesian practice reserved for non-combat units. The Police beret badge is of the same design as the centrepiece on the Police airborne wings worn over the left pocket. A Pelepor badge is worn on the right shoulder, a BRIMOB insignia and sub-unit designation tab on the left. The black Indonesian pistol belt, based on the US design, has a holstered 9mm Pindad (an Indonesian-made copy of the Beretta) on the right side. BRIMOB members wore the Indonesian spot camouflage pattern during the early 1960s (see C1); British DPM is now worn on jungle operations.

Indonesia:
E1: Commando, KIPAM, 1986

This KIPAM amphibious commando wears the newer issue British DPM camouflage pants with an older issue KIPAM camouflage jacket similar in pattern to the British Denison smock. A Korps Komando (Marine) beret badge is worn on the standard purple Marine beret. A Marine Corps insignia is worn on the right shoulder, the KIPAM unit insignia and tab on the left shoulder. Over the right pocket are a name tag and a cloth US Navy SEAL qualification badge; On the right side are KIPAM and KIPAM HALO qualification badges; to avoid overcrowding, Marine jumpwings have been omitted from the uniform. The 'Marines' tag over the pocket reflects the current practice of wearing service affiliation on the left breast.

Apart from specialized gear such as underwater swimming equipment, KIPAM commandos are outfitted with standard Marine Corps items. The AK-47 is the Marine weapon of choice due to its reliable reputation in muddy conditions. Also used by the KIPAM is the Belgian FNC made under licence in Indonesia.

SAF anti-terrorist team dressed in US leaf camouflage and armed with H&K assault rifles.

E2: Private, Detachment 81, 1989

After major re-organization of the Armed Forces in early 1986 all élite units were ordered to standardize with British DPM. KOPASSUS, however, still continues to use its older issue 'Special Forces Pattern' uniform during training cycles. The red beret, beret badge, and SF qualification badge have all remained identical since RPKAD days. The subdued unit shoulder insignia is also of the earlier design, except that the attached tab has changed from 'Para-Komando' to KOPASSUS. On the right shoulder, red numbered squares are used to distinguish Groups 1, 2, and 3; KOPASSUS HQ personnel and Detachment 81 commandos wear a red square with the letter 'M', an abbreviation for 'Headquarters' in Indonesian.

The Indonesian-made version of the Belgian FNC, seen here, and the US M-16 are current issue in KOPASSUS. Detachment 81 also uses the H&K MP5. British body armour was initially used by the detachment, with a modified version offering better crotch protection ordered after a serious casualty was sustained during the Woyla operation. German and US body armour are also used at present. Stun-grenades are imported from England.

E3: Major, KOSTRAD, 1989

All members of KOSTRAD wear a green beret with distinctive metal badge; those belonging to KOSTRAD airborne units add a small metal Army jumpwing to the front of the beret. A cloth KOSTRAD insignia (same design as the beret badge) and KOSTRAD tab are worn on the left shoulder. On occasion, a red tab bearing the battalion number is added above the KOSTRAD tab. Rank is worn on the shoulders, or, in this case, on a chest tab.

Philippines Special Forces insignia: chest qualification badge (left); unit shoulder insignia (right).

Thailand:
F1: Sergeant, Thai Special Forces, 1989
From 1957 to 1959 the Thai Airborne Rangers wore an olive drab beret; in 1959 a maroon beret was adopted, with a padded Royal Thai Army beret badge in both cloth and bullion versions. Despite the proliferation of unofficial insignia, the number of official insignia for the Thai SF is quite small. Subdued Army wings are worn above the left pocket; both domestic and foreign qualification badges, such as the subdued Ranger qualification badge seen here, go above the right pocket. Graduates of the LRRP course occasionally wear a triangular LRRP patch on the right pocket; distinctive insignia for the Special Warfare Command and Special Warfare Center are worn on the left pocket. (The insignia for the Special Warfare Command is seen on the sign in the background; the 'U' stands for 'Unconventional Warfare'.) Rank insignia, patterned after the US system, are worn on the shoulder, and subdued name tags occasionally over the right pocket.

The Thai SF have used literally dozens of camouflage patterns over the years, including several different copies of US leaf, British DPM, and US World War Two 'maple leaf' patterns. The Thai tiger-stripes seen here are one of the most common in the SF. In addition, olive drab fatigues in several styles are also issued. The magazine pouches and US-style pistol belt, suspenders, and jungle shoes are all of Thai manufacture. The M-16 is common issue in the Thai SF; also used are the CAR-15, H&K MP5, and Thai-made versions of the G-3 and H&K 33.

F2: Special Colonel, Thai SF, 1988
The Royal Thai Army has several different working and service dress uniforms, including long-sleeve brown shirt and slacks; olive drab short-sleeve shirt and slacks; olive drab jacket and slacks similar to the US Army; and dress whites. This Thai SF Special Colonel wears yet another version consisting of a short-sleeve white shirt and brown pants. A padded bullion Royal Thai Army badge is worn on the maroon beret. On the left pocket are bullion Thai Army jumpwings; over the pocket, metal US Army wings and a

metal Thai Army Ranger qualification badge. A badge awarded to Thai Army Command and Staff course graduates is on the right pocket. On the collar are metal infantry insignia; metal rank insignia are on the shoulders. British Army jumpwings are worn on the right shoulder. A black plastic name tag is occasionally worn over the right pocket.

F3: Captain, PARU, 1971
As the first élite airborne unit in Thailand, PARU adopted a distinctive black beret in the mid-1950s. No official beret badge existed, although photos from 1961 show PARU commandos wearing metal Police airborne wings on their berets. After the BPP received counter-insurgency training in the mid-1960s the entire BPP began wearing the black beret with metal BPP beret badge. PARU is now distinguished by a maroon beret flash.

The figure, based on a photograph of a PARU officer assigned to the Special Battalion at Phitsanulok, has broken normal rules of insignia placement: Thai Police wings and US jumpwings are worn over the left pocket; Thai Army jumpwings and Thai rigger wings are on the right. The badge on the right pocket is for graduates of the Royal Thai Army Command and Staff course. Rank insignia, similar to the US system, are worn on the right collar, a Police collar badge on the left collar. No official PARU unit insignia is worn. PARU is issued standard Thai Army weapons and equipment.

Thailand:
G1: NCO, Thai Air Force CCT, 1987
The Thai Air Force CCT wears a black beret with padded bullion Air Force insignia. On operations they are outfitted much like the Thai Army Special Forces. This man wears Thai tiger-stripes with US-style web gear. He carries a silenced H&K MP5; the unsilenced version is also used by the Team. Though not seen on this figure, members of the CCT often wear non-Air Force qualification badges, such as Marine Recon wings, over the right pocket.

G2: NCO, Thai Navy SEAL, 1989
The Royal Thai Navy SEALs currently wear a leaf camouflage uniform with matching beret. Active members of the SEAL Team wear the SEAL qualification badge on the left side; Navy jumpwings are shifted over to the right side to provide a balanced effect. (Qualifications which draw extra pay, such as the SEAL qualification, are worn on the left.) The standard SEAL weapon is the M-16.

G3: Lieutenant, Marine Recon, 1989
The RTMC Recon Battalion is issued US-style leaf camouflage. The matching US Marine camouflage cap has a Thai Marine Corps globe-and-anchor insignia stencilled on the front. The Recon Battalion insignia on the left shoulder features a skull with crossed oars. The current recon qualification badge is on the right side; Navy airborne wings are on the left. Subdued rank insignia, which were standardized for all Thai Armed Forces utility uniforms in late 1988, are worn on the collar.

Malaysia:
H1: NCO, MSSG, 1988
Since 1971 a distinctive Malaysian camouflage uniform has been worn on combat operations. Although a matching jungle hat is issued to other units of the Malaysian Army, the SF

normally wear their green beret on operations. The cap badge has been worn since the creation of the MSSR in 1970; it underwent slight modification in 1988 (see I3). Various beret flashes are worn to distinguish sub-units within the MSSG. A subdued name tag is worn over the right pocket. A subdued 'Gerakhas' (a contraction of 'Gerak K'has', or 'Special Service') is worn over the left pocket. Subdued jumpwings are over the left pocket. Officers wear British-style rank on the shoulders.

The US-style pistol belt, made in Malaysia, is normally worn with a commando dagger on the left side. The ammunition pouches and suspenders are made in Malaysia. In addition to the M-16 the MSSG uses the CAR-15, H&K 33, and G-3. The US-style jungle boots with anti-pungi sole protectors are made in Malaysia.

H2: Lieutenant, SWTC, 1983

MSSG working dress is standard Malaysian Army issue. To set apart the MSSG, a 'Gerakhas' ('Special Service') tab is worn on the left shoulder and light blue lanyard on the right shoulder. Until 1985 jumpwings were worn on the left shoulder; metal or bullion Malaysian Army wings are now worn over the left pocket; 8 Ranger Battalion wear identical wings with a red cloth background; foreign wings, such as those depicted from the US, go over the right pocket. A removable plastic name plate is worn over the right pocket.

H3: MSSG shoulder insignia

On green service dress uniforms members of the MSSG HQ and Special Warfare Training Centre wear the standard Army HQ insignia on the right shoulder and cloth MSSG panther's head insignia on the left shoulder; members of the MSSG combat regiments wear only the panther patch.

Malaysia:
I1: NCO, HANDAU, 1988

HANDAU commandos wear a light blue beret with MSSG beret badge on an Air Force flash (see I3). Malaysian camouflage fatigues are worn on operations, with subdued cloth wings over the left pocket. A HANDAU tab is occasionally worn over the left pocket; a name tag goes over the right. A light blue lanyard is worn on working and service dress. No other official HANDAU insignia are worn.

I2: Commando, PASKAL, 1988

PASKAL is identified by its purple beret with Navy beret badge (see I4). Malaysian camouflage fatigues are worn on operations; working and dress uniforms are standard Navy issue. Weapons and equipment are the same as for the MSSG. Subdued cloth Malaysian Army wings are worn over the left pocket of the combat uniform; metal wings are worn on service and dress uniforms. No other official Paskal insignia are worn.

I3: HANDAU beret badge

HANDAU wears the standard MSSG gold metal beret badge on a Royal Malaysian Air Force flash. The motto 'Chepat Dan Chergas' ('Quick and Active') was changed in 1988 to 'Cepat Dan Cerpas' following grammatical changes in the Malaysian language. During the same year slight changes were made to the panther's head after the King of Malaysia requested that it be made to look more ferocious.

Philippines Navy SWAG team practising amphibious infiltrations. They are dressed in an assortment of leaf camouflage and olive drab fatigues.

14: PASKAL beret badge

In deference to the training received from the MSSG, the initial cadre of PASKAL commandos wore the MSSG beret badge. Currently, the Royal Malaysian Navy cap badge in gold metal is worn as a beret badge. The inscription reads 'Allah and Muhammed'.

Philippines:

J1: Lieutenant, SWAG, 1984

Based on a 1984 photo, this SWAG commando wears a black knit balaclava, olive drab fatigues, and US web gear. A belt of M-60 ammunition is draped around the neck. As is standard Philippine military practice, the service affiliation is printed over the right pocket; name, rank and serial number are printed above the left pocket. These pocket tabs come in various colours, most often black printing on a light green background. On occasion, they are sewn in black thread

directly onto the uniform. Although SWAG unit insignia exists, it is not worn on the combat uniform.

J2: NCO, HDFG, 1978

In 1977 the HDFG began wearing the distinctive 'Seven Colours' camouflage uniform seen here. The rucksack is of indigenous manufacture. An 'Airborne' tab is worn on the left shoulder, a 'Ranger' tab on the right. Army wings are worn above the left pocket; above them is a cloth 'Mindinao Campaign' badge signifying a combat tour in the southern Philippines during the height of the Mindinao insurgency of the early 1970s.

J3: Staff Sergeant, SAF, 1986

During the February 1986 Revolution SAF commandos were pictured in a variety of camouflage uniforms, including US leaf, Philippine tiger-stripes, and Philippine leaf variants such as the one pictured here. A distinctive SAF winged sword metal beret badge is worn with a red flash on a black beret. A 'Special Action Force' tab is worn on the left shoulder, a 'Ranger' tab on the right shoulder. Cloth Constabulary jumpwings are worn over the left pocket. To distinguish anti-Marcos troops

Commanding Officer of Singapore's 1 Cdo. Bn. holding the 1987 Best Unit Award. He wears Singaporean and Israeli jumpwings. Note Thai Army jumpwings on several of the other officers. The Commandos wear a metal National Armed Forces insignia on red berets.

Vietnamese *Dac Cong* team dressed in green-based PAVN camouflage with matching soft caps, 1986.

from Marcos loyalists, rebel units such as the SAF wore the Philippine flag upside down, or else shifted it from the right shoulder to the left shoulder or left pocket.

Philippines:

K1: NCO, SAF, 1987

Since the 1986 February Revolution the SAF has occasionally been deployed on combat operations. On one such occasion, during the reinforcement of Bicol in 1987, a squad of well-equipped SAF commandos posed for publicity pictures. US leaf camouflage fatigues are worn with SAF black berets and metal SAF beret badges. A Philippine flag is worn on the right shoulder, with '*Special Action Force*' tabs on both shoulders. On occasion SAF unit insignia are worn on the left shoulder or right pocket. As with the rest of the Armed Forces, the CAR-15 assault rifle and M1956 web gear are of US origin. The initials '*AFP*' ('Armed Forces of the Philippines') have been stencilled across the suspenders. The rucksack is of indigenous manufacture.

K2: Sergeant, HDFG, 1987

In the mid-1980s the HDFG began to phase out the 'Seven Colours' camouflage in favour of US-style leaf camouflage. In late 1987 the HDFG stopped wearing camouflage and began issuing olive drab jungle fatigues. The HDFG sergeant depicted wears an olive drab beret with the current embroidered beret badge. On the left shoulder a '*Special Forces*' tab is correctly worn at the top, with an '*Airborne*' tab in the middle, and a subdued HDFG unit insignia (same design as the beret badge) at the bottom. On the left pocket is a Special Forces qualification badge; above the pocket are cloth Philippine Army jumpwings. On the right shoulder is an embroidered Philippine flag, officially replaced in mid-1988 by an embroidered seal of the Armed Forces of the Philippines.

K3: Sergeant, SRR, 1986

The Scout Rangers are renowned for their relaxed uniform code; modifications are in fact the norm rather than the exception. Taken from a photo, this sergeant wears an all-black fatigue uniform, the unofficial trademark of both the old and current Scout Ranger Regiments. Also common are olive drab fatigues and US leaf pattern camouflage. Insignia placement on this figure only partially follows official regulations. The '*Ranger*' tab is on the left shoulder and metal Ranger qualification badge (the same design used by the SRR in the 1950s) on the left pocket are correctly positioned. However, the Scout Ranger unit insignia normally placed on the left shoulder has been shifted to the right shoulder in place of the standard Philippine flag. The unit insignia is also occasionally seen on the right pocket.

The black beret is official issue to the Scout Rangers, a holdover from the SRR of the 1950s. The woven beret flash is of the same basic design as the unit shoulder insignia. Other insignia, such as the metal Ranger qualification badge, are occasionally worn as unofficial beret badges. The pistol belt and suspenders are of US origin; the rucksack is of indigenous manufacture. The weapon is a US M-14.

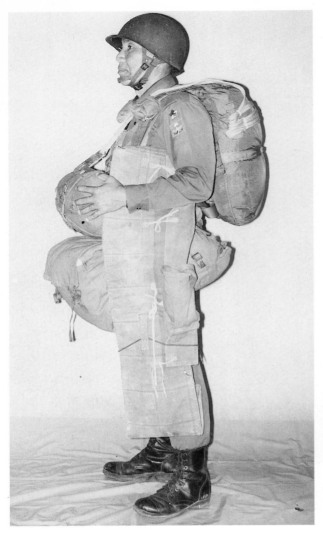

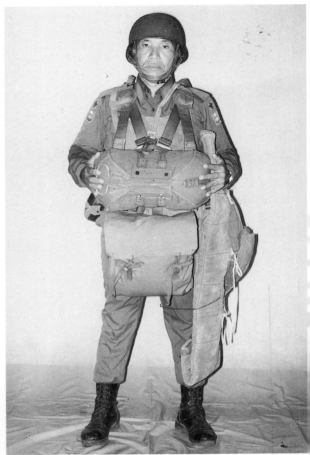

Two views of a Burmese paratrooper, 1989. Equipment consists of old US issue and South Korean-made copies. Metal sergeant's insignia are on the shoulders; below these is the cloth, Airborne Battalion patch. (Courtesy Myanmar Embassy, Washington)

People's Republic of Vietnam:
L1: Dac Cong paratrooper, 1985
This Vietnamese paratrooper, taken from a 1985 photo in the official Army journal, is one of six *Dac Cong* commandos boarding an An-2 for a training jump. He wears a ribbed Soviet paratrooper helmet and PAVN canvas and rubber combat shoes. The parachute is the Soviet D-5, with a Z-5 reserve on his chest. Camouflage has been in wide use among *Dac Cong* units since 1984. The green-based version seen here is issued to commando elements operating in jungle regions; a brown-based variant (see L2) is in use in dry regions such as those found in Cambodia. In addition, old ARVN Airborne leaf camouflage material has been re-cut into uniforms according to PAVN standards.

L2: Dac Cong Commando, 1986
From a 1986 photo in the official PAVN journal, this *Dac Cong* commando is identified as part of 302 Division, known to be operating in Siem Reap, Cambodia, at the time. He wears the short-sleeve, brown-based *Dac Cong* camouflage outfit with matching cap, appropriate for the dry terrain of north-western Cambodia. Because the *Dac Cong* operate primarily

on short-duration missions in conjunction with infantry sweeps, this commando is lightly equipped with only a Soviet AKMS.

L3: Dac Cong insignia
In January 1983 the PAVN began issuing new branch and specialist insignia. The *Dac Cong* wear collar insignia of thin stamped metal worn on red collar tabs bearing a dagger above a satchel charge. No distinctive insignia were previously worn by the *Dac Cong*.

L4: Parachute insignia
305 Parachute Brigade never developed its own distinctive jumpwings; not until 1982 were insignia created for para-qualified *Dac Cong* personnel. Parachute insignia were initially described in a January 1983 PAVN publication as 'an aircraft with a fully opened parachute'. In July 1983, they were described again as an 'aircraft wing with an opening para-chute'. When finally issued, the para insignia was of thin stamped metal worn on light blue collar tabs bearing an aircraft wing above an opened parachute.

Dac Cong practise martial arts techniques; they are dressed in PAVN camouflage with matching caps.

Notes sur les planches en couleur

A1 Béret LLDB, écusson de 1964; écusson LLDB sur l'épaule gauche; brevet LLDB au-dessus de la poche droite. **A2** écusson d'épaule LLDB, bottes Bata, sinon équipement courant de fabrication américaine. **A3** Béret et badge LLDN. L'écusson rouge sur la poche identifie les SEALS dans les LLDN; brevet SEAL vietnamien au-dessus de la poche droite, écusson de qualification SEAL de l'US Navy au-dessus de la poche gauche.

B1 Béret rouge STD avec écusson des unités aéroportées ARVN; uniforme des unités aéroportées ARVN et écussons en sus de l'écusson de dragon SMS sur l'épaule gauche, brevet sur l'épaule droite. **B2** Premier uniforme de camouflage des unités aéroportées, tel que le portèrent les unités conduites par des Français au début des années cinquante, avec insigne sur l'épaule gauche du Service de Liaison; écussons de qualification des unités aéroportées et de LRRP à gauche et à droite de la poitrine. **B3** Seule cette unité a conservé le béret vert après le démembrement du LLDB. Notez l'écusson sur l'épaule du Groupe de Chasseurs 81 aéroporté, sur le camouflage de "feuillage" de cet ARVN aéroporté.

C1 Uniforme de camouflage des Etats-Unis de style Seconde Guerre mondiale, avec écusson des Forces Spéciales de l'Aéronautique indonésenne sur l'épaule gauche, brevet sur l'épaule droite, le titre de l'unité à droite sur la poitrine; notez le fusil G3. **C2** Nouveau béret et écusson et nouveau camouflage de style belge uniques à cette unité. **C3** Un troisième modèle de camouflage fut brièvement adopté après que cette unité ait été renommée pour la seconde fois, et un nouvel écusson de béret. Les titres de l'unité à droite sur la poitrine furent alors remplacés par le nom du soldat. Notez l'insigne "peu voyant" des Forces Spéciales sur l'épaule gauche.

D1 Trois types de camouflage furent portés au début des années quatre-vingts par cette unité – un modèle ancine de "feuille" des Etats-Unis, un modèle à rayures veritcales sombres (comme sur la couverture du casque), et le modèle de style britannique (comme sur la veste) – dans des combinaisons variées. Notez

Farbtafeln

A1 LLDB Baskenmütze; 1964–Abzeichen; LLDB linker Schultertreifen; LLDB Flügelabzeichen über der rechten Tasche. **A2** LLDB Schulterabzeichen, Bata-Stiefel, sonst die standardmäßige amerikanische Ausrüstung. **A3** LLDN Baskenmütze und Abzeichen. Rotes Taschenabzeichen läßt die SEALS innerhalb der LLDN erkennen; vietnamesische SEAL Flügelabzeichen über der rechten Tasche, US Navy SEAL Qualifizierungsabzeichen über der linken Tasche.

B1 Rote STD-Baskenmütze mit ARVN Luftlandetruppen-Abzeichen; ARVN Luftlandetruppen-Uniform und-abzeichen mit Ausnahme des SMS Drachenabzeichens auf der linken Schulter. **B2** Anfängliche Luftlandetruppen-Tarnuniform, die von den französisch-geführten Einheiten in den frühen 50ern getragen wurden; auf der linken Schulter ist die Liaison Service- Insignie zu sehen; LRRP und Luftlandetruppen-Qualifikationsabzeichen auf der linken und rechten Brustseite. **B3** Nur diese Einheit behielt die grüne Baskenmütze nach der Auflösung der LLDB. Zu beachten ist das Schulterabzeichen der 81 Airborne Ranger Group auf dem ARVN Luftlandetruppen "Blatt"-Tarnzeug.

C1 Amerikanische Tarnuniform aus dem Zweiten Weltkrieg mit Abzeichen der Indonesian Air Force Special Force auf der linken Schulter sowie Flügelabzeichen auf der linken Brustseite und Einheitsbezeichnung auf der rechten Brustseite; zu beachten ist das G3 Gewehr. **C2** Neue Baskenmütze und Abzeichen sowie im belgischen Stil gehaltenes Tarnzeug, das nur bei dieser Einheit zu finden war. **C3** Ein drittes Tarnzeugmuster wurde nach der zweiten Umbenennung der Einheit mit einem neuen Baskenmützenabzeichen vorübergehend eingeführt. Zu beachten ist die "gedämpfte" Special Forces Gruppeninsignie auf der linken Schulter.

D1 Drei Tarnzeugstile wurde zu Beginn der 80er Jahre von dieser Einheit in verschiedenen Kombinationen getragen: das frühe amerikanische "Blatt"-Muster, das dunkle, vertikal-gestreifte Muster (auf dem Helmüberzug) und das

l'écusson KOSTRAD et le titre sur l'épaule gauche. **D2** Béret et écusson du RPKAD de 1958, uniforme de camouflage du RPKAD de 1964, insigne d'unité de Para-Komando sur l'épaule gauche, brevet "Armée" d'unités aéroportées et écusson de qualification des Forces Spéciales à gauche sur la poitrine. **D3** Usage peu courant du béret penchant à gauche, que l'on ne voyait que dans les unités qui ne participaient pas au combat. Ecusson sur le béret de la police et ailes sur la poitrine; écusson Pelepor (Chasseur) sur l'épaule droite, écusson Brimob (Brigade Mobile) et désignation de l'unité à gauche.

E1 Pantalons de distribution ancienne des KIPAM, veste britannique nouvellement distribuée de camouflage DPM, béret de fusilier marin et écusson; Insigne du Corps des Fusiliers marins sur l'épaule droite, insigne KIPAM à gauche; différents badges de qualification KIPAM et USN SEAL sur la poitrine. **E2** Le camouflage "modèle des forces spéciales" démodé, le béret rouge et le badge de qualification des Forces Spéciales sont encore utilisés, bien qu'officiellement toutes les unités de forces spéciales indonésiennes portent maintenant le camouflage britannique DPM en combat. Les carrés rouges sur l'épaule droite portent les numéros de groupe, ou "M" pour le quartier général et le Détachement 81. Notez le fusil FNC de fabrication locale. Une armure pour se protéger le corps britannique, des Etats-Unis et allemande est utilisée pendant les opérations. **E3** Béret et écusson KOSTRAD, portés avec le brevet Armée pour les unités aéroportées. L'écusson est répété en tissu sur l'épaule gauche, parfois sous une barre rouge portant le numéro du bataillon.

F1 Béret de 1959; brevet thaï et étranger et écussons de qualification à gauche et à droite sur la poitrine respectivement; le camouflage à rayures de tigre thaï est l'un des modèles les plus courants sur plusieurs modèles thaïs et étrangers. **F2** Mélange peu courant d'uniformes blanc et brun; béret courant des Forces Spéciales avec écusson Armée; brevet thaï et des Etats-Unis; badge de qualification des Chasseurs et (sur la poche droite) écusson de gradé des cours de l'Ecole d'Officiers sur la poitrine; notez également le brevet britannique sur la manche. **F3** Béret noir de la Police de la Frontière et écusson, avec piece de parachutiste rouge foncée.

G1 Béret et écusson de l'Aviation, autrement l'uniforme et l'equipement ressemble à celui de Forces Spéciales de l'Armée. Notez le Heckler & Koch MP5 silencieux. **G2** Béret et uniforme spécial de camouflage "à feuilles" des SEALS. **G3** Insigne du bataillon sur l'épaule gauche d'un uniforme au style très américain; badge de qualification de fusilier marin de reconnaissnace à droite sur la poitrine, écusson naval à gauche.

H1 Béret des Forces Spéciales avec uniforme de camouflage malais; plusieurs écussons de couleur distinguaient les unites mais toutes portaient l'écusson de calot des Forces Spéciales et la désignation Forces Spéciales à gauche sur la poitrine. **H2** Désignation sur l'épaule gauche des Forces Spéciales et aiguillette bleue pâle sur l'epaule droite identifiant le MSSR quand il est en uniforme standard de l'armée. **H3** Les régiments du groupe MSS portaient cet écusson sur l'épaule gauche.

I1 Ces commandos de l'Aéronautique portent l'écusson MSSG sur des bérets bleus clairs avec un écusson de l'Aéronautique. La désignation HANDAU fut quelquefois portée sur l'uniforme de camouflage malais, sur l'épaule gauche, et un nom sur la droite. **I2** Béret de commando naval, écusson de la marine, uniforme courant de l'armée, brevet, et équipement. **I3** Détail de l'écusson HANDAU du béret – écusson courant du Groupe MSS sur une pièce avec fond de l'Aéronautique. **I4** Ecusson PASKAL sur le béret de cette unité de la marine.

J1 Désignation de l'arme à droite sur la poitrine; nom, rang et numéro à gauche. Aucun insigne d'unité SWAG n'était porté sur l'uniforme de combat. **J2** Camouflage dit en "sept couleurs" de l'HDFG à partir de 1977; Titre "Aéroporté" sur l'épaule gauche, "Chasseur" sur la droite. Brevet de l'armée, à gauche sur la poitrine et écusson de la campagne de Mindanoa. **J3** Uniforme de fabrication locale, l'un des différents modèles de camouflage utilisés, avec béret SAF et écusson, titres "Force Spéciale d'Action" et "Chasseur" sur les épaules gauche et droite. Les troupes rebelles portaient un écusson aux couleurs nationales inversées, ou le firent passer du bras droit au gauche sur sur la poche.

K1 Uniforme et équipement US standard, avec béret SAF et insigne. **K2** Les HDFG changèrent en 1987 l'uniforme de camouflage US contre des uniformes verts unis. Des insignes HDFG sont brodés sur le béret et les désignations ci-dessous sur la manche. **K3** Les "Scout Rangers" sont connus pour avoir des uniformes de combat d'une grande variété; le noir est populaire. L'insigne de l'unité est porté ici par erreur sur l'épaule droite au lieu de la gauche; le béret noir de l'unité le même badge.

L1 Camouflage avec ombres vertes et marrons largement utilisé depuis 1984 dans les unités de Dac Cong; le parachute et le casque sont soviétiques. **L2** Soldat de la 302éme Division opérant au Cambodge, il porte l'uniforme de camouflage dont la couleur de fond est marron. **L3** Badge de col de 1983, porté sur un écusson rouge par le Dac Cong. **L4** Badge de 1983 de 1983 porté sur un écusson de col blue pâle par les troupes du Dac Cong qui ont reçu leur brevet de parachutisme.

britische Muster (auf der Jacke). Auffallend ist das KOSTRAD-Abzeichen und -Bezeichnung auf der linken Schulter. **D2** RPKAD-Baskenmütze und -Abzeichen von 1958, RPKAD-Tarnuniform von 1964, Fallschirmjäger-kommando-Einheitsinsignie auf der linken Schulter; Flügelabzeichen der Luftlandetruppen der Armee und Special Forces Qualifikationsabzeichen auf der linken Brustseite. **D3** Ungewöhnliche Verwendung der nach links zeigenden Baskenmütze. Mankonnte dies sonst nur bei Einheiten sehen, die nicht kämpften. Polizei-Baskenmützen-Abzeichen und Brustflügelabzeichen; Pelepor (Ranger) - Abzeichen auf der rechten Schulter, Brimob (Mobile Brigade) – Abkürzung, die auf dem Abzeichen angebracht und links davon mit der Einheitskennzeichnung versehen war.

E1 Alte Ausgabe der KIPAM Hosen, Neuausgabe der britischen DPM-Tarnjacke, Marine-Baskenmütze und -Abzeichen; Marine Corps-Insignie auf der rechten Schulter, KIPAM-Insignie links; verschiedene KIPAM und USN SEAL Qualifikations-Abzeichen auf der Brust. **E2** Veraltete Tarnbekleidung im Muster der "Sondereinheiten", rote Baskenmütze und Qualifikationsab-zeichen der Special Forces werden immer noch verwendet, obgleich alle indonesischen Sondereinheiten nunmehr britische DPM-Tarnbekleidung im Einsatz tragen. Rote Quadrate auf der rechten Schulter besitzen Gruppennum-mern oder "M", was Hauptquartier und Abteilung 81 bedeutet. Bemerkens-wert sind die selbst hergestellten FNC Gewehre. Britischer, amerikanischer und deutscher Körperschutz wird bei Einsätzen getragen. **E3** KOSTRAD-Baskenmütze und -Abzeichen, die zusammen mit kleinen Armee-Flügelabzeichen der Luftlandeeinheiten getragen wurden. Das Abzeichen wurde im Stoff auf der linken Schulter wiederholt. Gelegentlich war es unter der rechten Klappe mit der Bataillonsnummer zu sehen.

F1 Baskenmütze aus dem Jahre 1959. Thailändische und ausländische Flügel-und Qualifikationsabzeichen auf der linken und rechten Brustseite; thailändi-sche Tigerstreifen-Tarnbekleidung ist eine der häufig benutzten ausländischen und thailändischen Muster. **F2** Eine ungewöhnliche Mischung aus weißen und braunen Uniformen; in der Regel Special Forces-Baskenmütze mit Armeeab-zeichen; thailändische und amerikanische Flügelabzeichen, thailändisches Ranger-Qualifikationsabzeichen auf der Brust. Zu bemerken sind ebenso die britischen Flügelabzeichen auf dem Ärmel. **F3** Schwarze Baskenmütze der Border Police mit Abzeichen und kastianenbraunes PARU-Abzeichen.

G1 Baskenmütze und Abzeichen der Air force; die restliche Uniform und Ausrüstung ist der der Army Special Forces ähnlich. Auffallend ist die schallgedämpfte Heckler & Koch MP5. **G2** Besondere Baskenmütze im "Blatt"-Tarnmuster sowie Uniform der SEAL. **G3** Bataillionsinsignie auf der linken Schulter einer sehr im amerikanischen Stil gehaltenen Uniform. Reconnaissance Marines Qualifikations-Abzeichen auf der rechten Brustseite, Marineflügelzeichen links.

H1 Baskenmütze der Special Forces mit malaysischer Tarnuniform; ver-schiedene Farbabzeichen unterscheiden die Einheiten, alle tragen jedoch das Mützenabzeichen der Special Forces und deren linke Brustseiten-Kennzeichnung. **H2** Linke Schulterkennzeichnung der Special Forces und hellblaue, rechte Schulterkordel zur Erkennung der MSSR in der standardmäßigen Armee-Uniform. **H3** MSS Gruppenregimenter tragen dieses linke Schulterabzeichen.

I1 Diese Air Force-Kommandos tragen das MSSG-Abzeichen auf hellblauen Baskenmützen mit dem Aïr Force-Abzeichen. HANDAU-Kennzeichnung wurde manchmal auf der linken Brustseite der malaysischen Tarnuniform getragen und der Name auf der rechten. **I2** Baskenmütze des Naval Com-mando, Marineabzeichen, standardmäßige Army-Uniform, Flügelabzeichen und Ausrüstung. **I3** Teilausschnitt eines HANDAU Baskenmützenausschnitts – standardmäßiges MSS Gruppenabzeichen der Air Force Futterabzeichen. **I4** PASKAL Einheitsbaskenmützenabzeichen der Navy.

J1 Dienstbezeichnung auf der rechten Brustseite, Name, Rang und Dienst-nummer auf der linken Brustseite. Auf der Kampfuniform wurden keine SWAG Einheitsinsignien getragen. **J2** "Siebenfarbiges" Tarnzeug der HDFG aus dem Jahre 1977; "Luftlandetruppen"-Bezeichnung auf der linken Schulter, "Ran-ger" auf der rechten. Auf der linken Brustseite, Army-Flügelabzeichen und das Mindanao Campaign Abzeichen aus den 70er Jahren. **J3** Am Ort hergestellte Uniform, wobei einer der verschiedene Tarnmuster benutzt wurde, mit SAF-Basken-mütze und -Abzeichen. "Special Action Force"- und "Ranger"-Bezeichnungen sind auf der linken undrechten Schulter zu sehen. Die rebellischen Truppen trugen ein umgekehrtes, nationales Flaggenzeichen, oder sie trugen es nicht auf dem rechten, sondern auf dem linken Arm oder auf der Tasche.

K1 Standardmäßige amerikanische Uniform mit SAF -Baskenmütze und-Insignie. **K2** Im Laufe von 1987 veränderte sich die HDFG von amerikanischen Tarn- auf schlichte, grüne Uniformen. Die HDGF-Insignie ist auf die Baskenmützen und unter der Armkennzeichnung gestickt. **K3** Scout Rangers sind für die großen Uniformsunterschiede bekannt. Schwarz ist beliebt. Die Einheitsinsignie wurde hier verkehrt getragen; auf der rechten, anstelle der linken Schulterseite. Die schwarze Einheitsbasenmütze besaß das gleiche Abzeichen.

L1 Seit 1984 wird bei den Dac Cong Einheiten ein in Grün- und Brauntönen gehaltenes Tarnmuster häufig getragen; der Fallschirm und der Helm stammen aus der Sowjetunion. **L2** Soldaten der 302 Division im Einsatz in Kambodscha. Sie tragen eine braune Tarnuniform. **L3** Kragenabzeichen aus dem Jahre 1983 wurden von den Dac Cong auf dem roten Streifen getragen. **L4** Abzeichen aus dem Jahre 1983 wurden auf dem hellblauen Kragenstreifen der qualifizierten Fallschirmtruppen der Dac Cong getragen.